AMIGURUMI Fairies

Landauer Publishing

Amigurumi Fairies

Landauer Publishing, *https://landauer.foxchapelpublishing.com*, is an imprint of Fox Chapel Publishing Company, Inc.

Project Team

Editorial Director: Brian Hurley

Acquisitions Editor: Amelia Johanson

Technical Editor: Therese Chynoweth

Editor: Christa Oestreich

Designer: Leslie Hall

Photographer: Mike Mihalo

Proofreader & Indexer: Gretchen Bacon

ISBN 978-1-63981-153-3

Library of Congress Control Number: 2026935239

Shutterstock used: Dmitr1ch (wood background: used throughout), ArtKio (knit background: used throughout), WindNoise (cloud background: used throughout), Achira22 (clouds and stars: 6–7), YZ vector (paper clip: 8, 11, 19, 33, 43, 60, 94, 128), macondofotografcisi (crochet hooks: 12), Melica (green and blue yarn: 14, 46, 120–121), Nataliia K (purple yarn: 14, 121), Ewa Studio (yarn: 126)

To learn more about the other great books from Fox Chapel Publishing, or to find a retailer near you, call toll-free at 800-457-9112 or visit us at www.FoxChapelPublishing.com.

We are always looking for talented authors.

To submit an idea, please send a brief inquiry to acquisitions@foxchapelpublishing.com.

Or write to:

Fox Chapel Publishing

903 Square Street

Mount Joy, PA 17552

Printed in China

First printing

AMIGURUMI *Fairies*

50 Patterns for Customizable Dolls and Magical Friends

AMBER BEAULIEU

Table of Contents

24
56
92
30
64
100
38
74
106
48
84

Meet the Fairies and Their Friends!

Hidden just beyond the world we see is a small, peaceful realm where magic is simply part of everyday life. Here, fairies work together to keep nature running smoothly, from the change of the seasons to the glow of the night sky. It's a place full of tiny homes tucked into tree roots, lanterns made of firefly light, and soft paths where unicorns wander alongside their fairy friends.

In this book, you'll meet the fairies who help keep nature in balance. Get to know the seasonal fairies, who guide spring, summer, autumn, and winter to secretly keep our world on track. Discover the woodland fairies, who care for the forests, mushrooms, and small creatures that depend on them. Look up at the celestial fairies, who make sure the stars shine, the moon glows, and the night feels safe. Alongside them are their cheerful helpers—toads, fireflies, and unicorn companions—each adding their own touch of magic.

As you crochet each character, you'll bring a little piece of this hidden realm to life. Every fairy has a role, a personality, and a bit of charm to share. So get cozy, gather your yarn, and with every stitch, tell the story of the fairies who magically keep our world running.

How to Use This Pattern Book

Welcome to your very own collection of fairy doll amigurumi patterns! This book is designed to allow you to create countless unique fairy dolls from a variety of versatile patterns.

USING MASTER PATTERNS

The master patterns in Chapter 3 serve as the foundation for creating every fairy doll in this collection. These patterns include the head, body, arms, legs, hair wig, and wings that form the core of each doll. You will be utilizing these patterns repeatedly as the starting point for each fairy.

Simply follow the master patterns to create your doll's basic shape, then customize your fairy's characteristics and style based on the pattern of your choice.

WINGS

Each fairy is designed to have posable wings, crocheted with a hidden craft wire that allows them to remain in a fixed position or bent into your own pose.

MIX AND MATCH

Each fairy doll pattern in this book is completely interchangeable. Love the style of the Forest Fairy's hair but prefer it on the Spring Fairy? Simply combine them! Every hairstyle can be paired with any doll foundation, giving you endless possibilities to create your very own unique fairy.

Color It Your Way

Do not feel limited by the suggested yarn colors in each pattern. The color possibilities are as limitless as your imagination!

SKILL LEVELS

These patterns assume you have acquired a basic understanding of crochet and you are comfortable with the fundamental stitches and techniques. Along with skill levels, each pattern includes instructions and stitch counts to support your crocheting journey. A stitch glossary and crochet abbreviations can be found in Chapter 7 as a handy reference.

Each pattern is marked with one of the following skill levels:

- **Sprinkle**—Simple pattern with minimal moving components and straightforward construction.

- **Shimmer**—Moderate pattern with shaping techniques and a few additional elements.

- **Sparkle**—Most intricate pattern with multiple pieces, complex assembly, and embellishments that create more detailed results.

An alternative solution to using safety eyes is to replace them with embroidered eyes.

SAFETY NOTICE

All fairies are designed for children ages five and up due to small parts that may present a choking hazard. The doll safety eyes, while securely attached, are small enough to potentially loosen with wear and tear.

Chapter 2

Amigurumi Essentials

Before you begin stitching your fairies and friends, it is helpful to gather the materials and tools that you will need to bring each character to life.

This chapter covers the essential yarns, tools, and craft supplies used throughout the book, along with a few personal recommendations that I think make constructing the characters both easier and unique. Using the suggested materials will help you achieve the size, structure, and finished piece shown in the patterns.

Once you gather the essentials, you can confidently substitute materials as you see fit and make each fairy and friend your own.

YARN

A #2 fine yarn is a good, lightweight option for amigurumi since it allows for delicate yet detailed work.

All patterns in this book are designed using #2 fine (sport) weight yarn. It's recommended to use the same weight, as lightweight yarn will make a big difference in achieving the same look as the dolls in this book.

The projects in this book use YarnArt Jeans yarn (1.76 oz [50g]/174 yds [160m]), a cotton-acrylic blend that shapes your designs exceptionally well while maintaining structure and durability. The yarn holds its form beautifully for amigurumi work. YarnArt Jeans is reasonably priced and readily available online, making it easy to stock up on a variety of colors. The quality and range of colors will ensure your work looks exactly as intended for these patterns; however, you can still use the yarn of your choice and closely match them to the colors suggested in the patterns.

Stitch markers are perfect for tracking rounds and specific stitches that you need to align to.

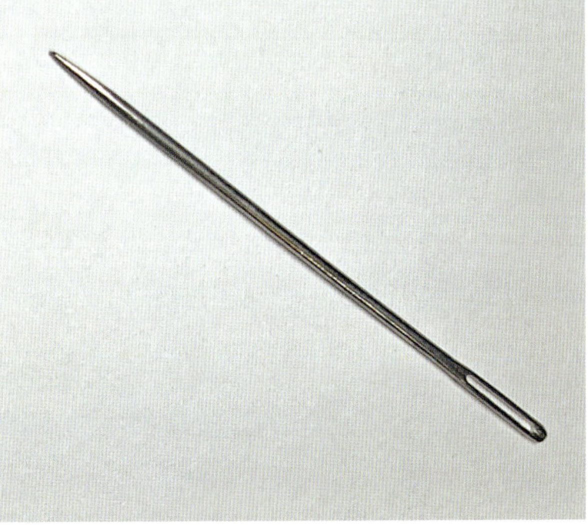

Tapestry needles help easily weave in yarn tails, sew, and even work embroidery stitches.

CROCHET TOOLS

- **Crochet Hooks**—Crochet hooks bring everything together; each stitch is formed by pulling yarn through loops to build the tight design of the pattern. The smaller hooks keep a better structure to the design and keep stitches firm and tightly woven together. Size US C/2 (2.75mm), US B/1 (2mm), and US 8/7/2 (1.5mm) hooks are used in patterns throughout the book.
- **Stitch Markers**—Stitch markers are used to help keep track of rounds, increases, decreases, or centering areas. They are optional, but having one handy can save time and prevent missed stitches.
- **Tapestry Needle**—A tapestry needle is used for sewing pieces together, closing openings, and weaving in ends with nearly invisible finishes. A blunt tip works best.
- **Small Embroidery Scissors**—Embroidery scissors make it easy to trim ends neatly and precisely, giving you more control when you are finishing your pieces. You can also use these to cut the thin wire used throughout this book.

Gauge

Gauge will naturally vary from maker to maker, and these patterns are written with that flexibility in mind. Feel free to size your hook up or down to suit your personal tension—the goal is not to hit the exact stitch count per inch but to achieve a dense, tightly stitched structure, where the stuffing stays hidden and the finished piece holds its shape.

BASIC CRAFT SUPPLIES

- **Jewelry Wire**—1⁄64" (4mm) wide or 26 gauge is used for creating the posable wings on your fairies. This can be purchased at most local craft stores or online.
- **Pipe Cleaners, Crafting Wire, or Flexible Foam Curling Rods**—Any one of these materials is essential for holding your doll's head in place. All patterns in this book use 3⁄8" (1cm) thick flexible foam curling rods because they easily hold the weight of the doll's head and even allow you to position the head in specific ways without losing structure. To see an example of using wire to hold the head, see page 18.
- **Clear Mini Hair Elastics**—These tiny elastic bands, often called polybands, are wonderful for making creations that your doll can hold and place on their wrist.
- **Doll Safety Eyes**— Safety eyes are two pieces of hard plastic: one rounded end with a screw and a piece to attach to the back. They are designed to lock into place, preventing them from pulling out of the piece over time. This provides the doll with a clean and consistent look for the characters' facial features. Install them before the piece is fully closed and stuffed, and then check the placement for the symmetry you are looking for—any small adjustments easily change the expression. See page 9 for an alternative option. 6mm safety eyes are used in each pattern except for the toad, which uses 9mm safety eyes.
- **Polyester Fiber Filling Doll Stuffing**—Firm, even stuffing helps maintain shape and structure without distorting the stitches. Polyester fiber fill is used to stuff all pieces in this book. It is usually made of 100% polyester fiber and comes hypoallergenic. Buy any choice you feel comfortable using.

Tip

Avoid using glue or fabric glue for eyes, as it can damage the yarn, seep through the stitches, and loosen or fall off over time.

Flexible foam curling rods are a good option for holding your doll's head in place.

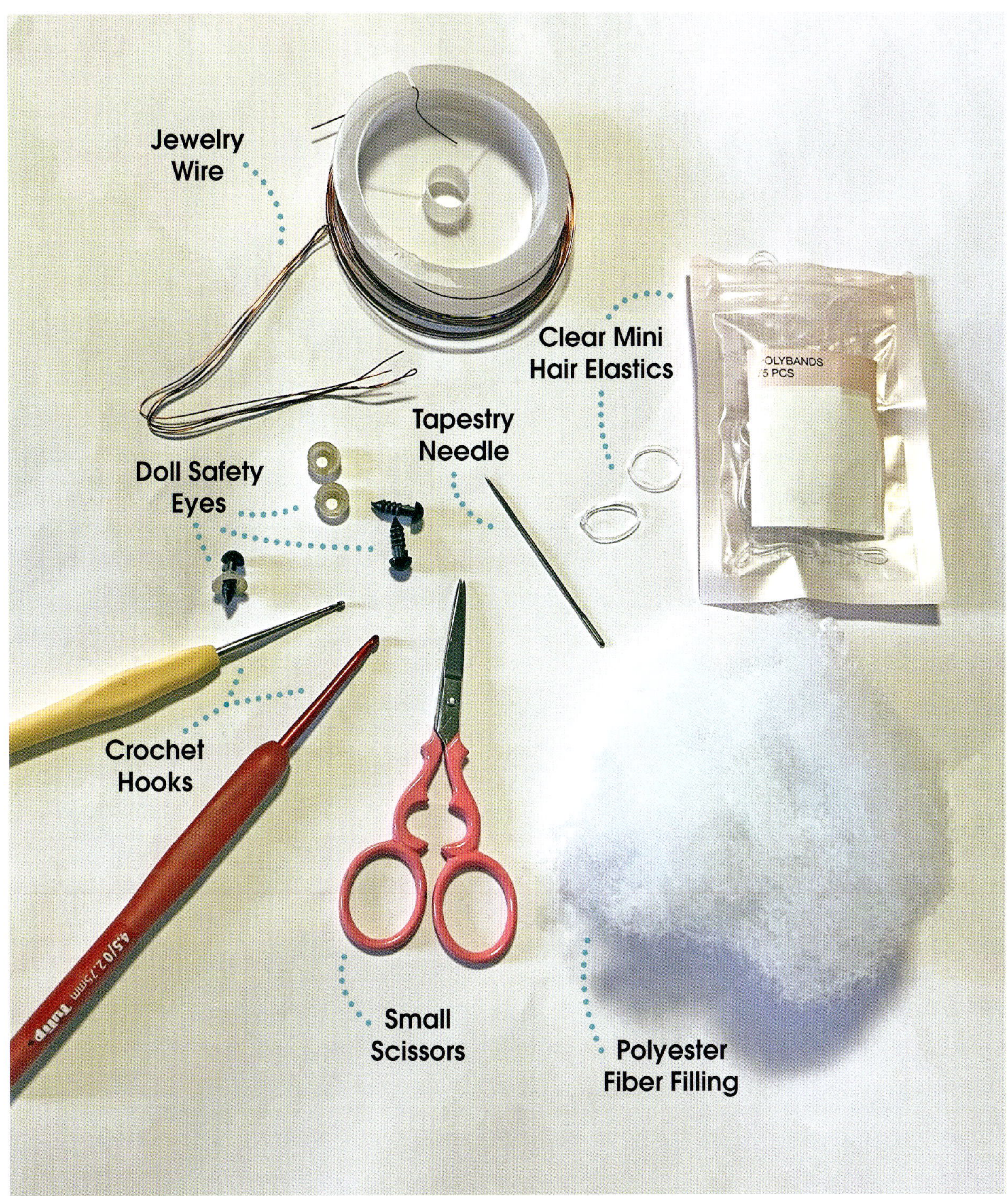

All the necessary tools you need! These projects don't require too much.

Chapter 3

Master Patterns

The patterns shown here are the structural foundation for every fairy character in this book. Think of the Fairy Doll Pattern as a shared base that establishes consistency and scale yet leaves room for customization through hairstyles, clothing, and wings. Once you become familiar with this pattern, you will find it easy to move from one character to another. Using the master pattern will also ensure that all your fairies stand together as one collection, yet each has her own personality and unique qualities.

Fairy Doll Pattern

The master fairy doll pattern is an adaptable base design used in all the fairy patterns within this book. Use this foundational pattern as a starting point for each unique character and adapt it accordingly to the pattern.

Finished Height:

- 9" (22.9cm)

Tools and Materials:

- US C/2 (2.75mm) crochet hook
- Scissors
- Tapestry needle
- Two 6mm safety eyes
- Polyester fiber filling
- Flexible foam curling rod

Yarn:

- YarnArt Jeans (Weight: #2 Fine)
    - Color 03 (Polar White)—1 ball
    - Color 73 (Peach) or Color 70 (Cocoa)—1 ball

Pattern Notes:

- These materials and yarn are standard for each fairy doll pattern. Refer to your chosen character's pattern for directions on specific color variations and use.
- Rounds are joined and not crocheted in spirals, unless otherwise specified. At the end of each round, join with a slip stitch in the first stitch of that round, then chain 1.

ARM (MAKE 2)

Fig. 1

Stuffing the Arm as you progress through the rounds to make it easier, start with the color peach or cocoa:

Round 1: 6 sc into a MR. [6 sts]

Round 2: (1 sc, 1 sc inc) 3 times. [9 sts]

Round 3: 1 sc in each st. [9 sts]

Round 4: 3 sc, 1 sc dec, 4 sc. [8 sts]

Rounds 5–16: 1 sc in each st. [8 sts]

Flatten the Arm and crochet 3 sc through both layers to close the Arm. Fasten off and weave in the yarn inside the Arm (*Fig. 1*).

The front of the Arm is indicated by the decrease created in Round 4.

LEG (MAKE 2)

Fig. 2

Fig. 3

Stuffing the Leg as you progress through the rounds, start with the color suggestion from your character's pattern:

Round 1: 6 sc into a MR. [6 sts]

Round 2: 1 sc inc in each st. [12 sts]

Rounds 3–5: 1 sc in each st. [12 sts]

Round 6: 4 sc, 2 sc dec, 4 sc. [10 sts]

Rounds 7–8: 1 sc in each st (*Fig. 2*), changing the color to peach or cocoa at the end of Round 8. [10 sts]

Round 9: BLO 1 sc in each st. [10 sts]

Rounds 10–20: 1 sc in each st. [10 sts]

Fasten off and weave in the yarn inside the Leg at the end of Round 20 for both Legs (*Fig. 3*). Do not flatten and crochet them closed as you did for the Arms.

Fig. 4

Fig. 5

Fig. 6

Fig. 7

BODY

Stuffing the Body as you progress through the rounds, start with the color polar white:

Attach a sl st to the inner thigh of the 1st Leg, ch 2, and attach to the inner thigh of the 2nd Leg with 1 sc. This is now the starting point of each round going forward.

Round 1: 9 sc around the 2nd Leg, 2 sc in the ch, 10 sc, around the 1st Leg, 2 sc in the opposite side of the ch (*Figs. 4 and 5*). [24 sts]

Round 2: (2 sc, 1 sc inc) 8 times. [32 sts]

Rounds 3–6: 1 sc in each st, change to the color suggestion of your character's pattern at the end of Round 6. [32 sts]

Round 7: (2 sc, 1 sc dec) 8 times. [24 sts]

Round 8: BLO 1 sc in each st. [24 sts]

Rounds 9–10: 1 sc in each st (*Fig. 6*). [24 sts]

Round 11: (1 sc, 1 sc dec) 8 times. [16 sts]

Rounds 12–14: 1 sc in each st. [16 sts]

Insert the Arms on this round, making sure they are facing correctly:

Round 15: 3 sc, 3 sc through the Arm connecting it with this round, 5 sc, 3 sc through the 2nd Arm (*Fig. 7*), 2 sc changing to the color peach or cocoa at the end of the round. [16 sts]

Round 16: BLO 1 sc in each st. [16 sts]

Round 17: 8 sc dec. [8 sts]

Do not fasten off.

HEAD

Continue from the pattern of the Body:

Round 1: 1 sc in each st. [8 sts]

Round 2: 1 sc inc in each st. [16 sts]

Round 3: (1 sc, 1 sc inc) 8 times. [24 sts]

Round 4: (1 sc inc, 2 sc) 8 times. [32 sts]

Round 5: (3 sc, 1 sc inc) 8 times. [40 sts]

Insert a foam curling rod (see box on page 19), or crafting wire as shown, through the Head down into the body to provide stability (*Fig. 8*). Stuff around the wire and stuff the Head as you progress through the rounds.

Round 6: (9 sc, 1 sc inc) 4 times. [44 sts]

Fig. 8

Fig. 9

Rounds 7–16: 1 sc in each st. [44 sts]

Insert the eyes between Rounds 9 and 10, approximately 8 stitches apart.

Round 17: (9 sc, 1 sc dec) 4 times. [40 sts]

Round 18: (3 sc, 1 sc dec) 8 times. [32 sts]

Round 19: (2 sc, 1 sc dec) 8 times. [24 sts]

Round 20: (1 sc, 1 sc dec) 8 times. [16 sts]

Round 21: 8 sc dec. [8 sts]

Fasten off and weave in the yarn inside the Head (*Fig. 9*).

Using Foam Curling Rods as a Head Stabilizer

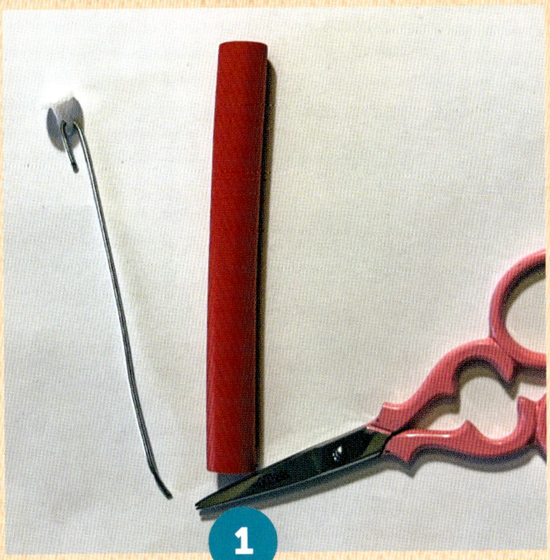

1 Cut a curling rod in half or between 3" (7.6cm) and 3½" (8.9cm) long. This includes the wire inside the rod.

2 Insert the rod into the neck before attaching the Head.

HAIR WIG

Fig. 10

Start with the color suggestion from your character's pattern:

Round 1: 6 sc in MR. [6 sts]

Round 2: 1 sc inc in each st. [12 sts]

Round 3: (1 sc, 1 sc inc) 6 times. [18 sts]

Round 4: (2 sc, 1 sc inc) 6 times. [24 sts]

Round 5: (1 sc inc, 3 sc) 6 times. [30 sts]

Round 6: 3 sc, 1 sc inc (4 sc, 1 sc inc) 5 times, 1 sc. [36 sts]

Round 7: (8 sc, 1 sc inc) 4 times. [40 sts]

Round 8: (9 sc, 1 sc inc) 4 times. [44 sts]

Rounds 9–19: 1 sc in each st (*Fig. 10*). [44 sts]

Do not sew the Hair Wig to the Head at this stage. Continue to work the piece using your character's pattern.

Special Guide for Fairy Wings

Each fairy has a specific pattern designed for their primary wings. However, this section outlines the structural approach for the primary wings and the shared pattern for the secondary wings. The primary wings work crochet stitches around a wire to hold their structure and pose them, yet they shape differently, so each fairy can showcase her unique qualities.

Unlike the primary wings, you will use the same master pattern to make the secondary wings. You do not use jewelry wire for these.

PRIMARY WINGS

Each pattern instructs you to make a crochet stitch around the wire to wrap it and secure it in place. Follow these instructions to learn how:

1

Cut a 32" (81.3cm) piece of wire and fold it in half. Once folded, it should measure approximately 16" (40.6cm).

2

Start with the color suggestion from your character's pattern. Work the first stitch through the looped end of the wire to anchor it to the wing.

3

Hold the wire in place, pull a loop up from under both strands of the wire, and finish the stitch above the wire.

Fig. 11

Fig. 12

SECONDARY WINGS

Using the following pattern and the color suggestion located in your character's pattern, crochet the Secondary Wings in rows:

Row 1: Ch 7, starting in the 2nd ch from the hook, 6 sc, ch 1, turn. [6 sts]

Row 2: 1 hdc inc, 4 hdc, 1 hdc inc, ch 1, turn. [8 sts]

Row 3: 1 hdc in each st, ch 1, turn. [8 sts]

Row 4: 1 hdc inc, 6 hdc, 1 hdc inc, ch 1, turn. [10 sts]

Rows 5–7: 1 hdc in each st, ch 1, turn. [10 sts]

Row 8: 1 hdc dec, 6 hdc, 1 hdc dec, ch 1, turn. [8 sts]

Row 9: 1 hdc dec, 4 hdc, 1 hdc dec, ch 1, turn. [6 sts]

Row 10: 1 hdc dec, 2 hdc, 1 hdc dec, ch 1, turn. [4 sts]

Row 11: 2 hdc dec, ch 1, do not turn. [2 sts]

EDGING

Rotate your work to the right. Along the edge, work 15 sc to the foundation ch, 6 sc along the bottom of the foundation ch, 15 sc along the other side edge, and join to the 1st hdc dec with a sl st (*Figs. 11 and 12*).

Fasten off and sew to the base of your fairy's wings unless otherwise stated in your character's pattern.

Fairies of the Seasons and Their Unicorn Friends

These fairies and unicorn friends bring their own personality, activities, and stories to the specific season they guard. Each fairy is connected to a specific season, and their designs reflect the unique look and feel of the time. Their unicorn friends share in their seasonal work, helping them with each activity they share. Together, these fairies and their companions bring the seasons to life, each adding their own playful magic and seasonal detail.

CHAPTER 4

Poppy the Summer Fairy

SKILL LEVEL: SPRINKLE

Poppy is the summer fairy who brings warm colors to the sky and a bit of sparkle to the waves. She can often be found along the shore, chatting with starfish and enjoying the ocean breeze. Poppy makes sure every summer day by the sea feels bright, fun, and full of life.

Finished Height:
- 9" (22.9cm)

Tools and Materials:
- US C/2 (2.75mm) crochet hook
- Two 6mm safety eyes
- Basic Craft Supplies (page 12)
- Basic Crochet Tools (page 11)

Yarn:
- YarnArt Jeans (Weight: #2 Fine)
  - Color 73 (Peach)—1 ball
  - Color 03 (Polar White)—1 ball
  - Color 07 (Tan)—1 ball
  - Color 11 (Pastel Green)—1 ball
  - Color 67 (Baby Chick)—1 ball
  - Color 05 (Ecru)—1 ball
  - Color 79 (Sea Green)—1 ball
  - Color 23 (Peace)—1 ball
- YarnArt Jeans Crazy (Weight: #2 Fine)
  - Color 8202 (1 ball)—Variegated

Pattern Notes:
- Follow the master fairy doll pattern (page 15) first before continuing with this pattern, using the following colors:
  - Arms/Legs/Head—peach
  - Hair Wig—baby chick
  - Body—polar white and peach
- Rounds are joined and not crocheted in spirals. At the end of each round, join with a slip stitch in the first stitch of that round, then chain 1.
- If instructed to cut a piece of yarn, use 36" (91.4cm) unless otherwise stated.

HAIR

Picking up from Round 19 of the Hair Wig, move on to Round 20. Round 20 will create Poppy's hairstyle. Continue with the same color (baby chick):

Round 20:

- **Part 1**—11 hdc, 1 sc.
- **Part 2 (First Braid)**—(ch 18, starting in the 2nd ch from the hook, 17 sl st) 3 times.
- **Part 3**—1 sc, 1 hdc, ch 6, starting in the 2nd ch from the hook, 2 sc in each ch, 1 sc, ch 3, starting from the 2nd ch from the hook 2 sc in each ch, 1 sc, 1 sl st.
- **Part 4 (First Hair Part)**—1 sc, 1 dc, 1 dc inc, 1 dc, 1 hdc, 1 sc, 3 sl st.
- **Part 5 (Second Hair Part)**—1 sc, 1 hdc, 1 dc, 1 dc inc, 1 dc, 1 hdc, 1 sc, 1 sl st.
- **Part 6**—ch 3, starting in the 2nd ch from the hook 2 sc in each ch, 1 sc, ch 6, starting in the 2nd ch from the hook, 2 sc in each ch, 2 hdc.
- **Part 7 (Second Braid)**—(ch 18, starting in the 2nd ch from the hook, 17 sl st) 3 times, join to the 1st hdc.

Fasten off and leave a long tail for sewing the Hair to the Head.

Sew the Hair Wig to the Head. Make two Braids with the strands of hair. Use a 2" (5.1cm) piece of pastel green yarn to tie the ends together with a tiny bow.

Fig. 1

Fig. 2

DRESS

You will start working the Dress in rows and then change to working in rounds. Starting with the variegated yarn:

Row 1: Ch 29, starting in the 2nd ch from the hook, 28 sc, ch 1, turn.

Row 2: 27 FPsc, 1 sc in the last st, ch 1, turn (*Fig. 1*). [28 sts]

Row 3: BLO, 1 sc in each st, ch 1, turn. [28 sts]

Row 4: Repeat Row 2. [28 sts]

Row 5: Repeat Row 3. [28 sts]

Row 6: BLO, 1 hdc inc, 26 hdc, 1 hdc inc, ch 1, turn. [30 sts]

Row 7: 1 hdc in each st, join with a sl st to the 1st hdc at the beginning of the row, ch 1 (*Fig. 2*). [30 sts]

You will now work in rounds.

Round 8: 1 hdc in each st, join to the 1st st, ch 1, do not turn. [30 sts]

Rounds 9–19: 1 hdc in each st, join to the 1st st, ch 1, do not turn. [30 sts]

Round 20: 1 sl st in each st.

Fasten off. The top half of the Dress should remain open for the Wings.

DRESS STRAPS

Continuing with the variegated yarn:

Step 1: Sl st to the last sc of Row 1, ch 7.

Step 2: 1 sc into sts 14 and 15 of Row 1 (center of the front of the Dress).

Step 3: Ch 7, sl st to the 1st sc of Row 1.

SHELL

Starting with the color tan: Ch 2, 5 sc into the 1st ch, fasten off, and attach to the center front of the Dress at the point of the Dress Straps.

Place the Dress on the doll.

HAT

Start with the color tan:

Round 1: 6 sc in MR. [6 sts]

Round 2: 1 sc inc in each st. [12 sts]

Round 3: (1 sc, 1 sc inc) 6 times. [18 sts]

Round 4: (2 sc, 1 sc inc) 6 times. [24 sts]

Round 5: (3 sc, 1 sc inc) 6 times. [30 sts]

Round 6: (4 sc, 1 sc inc) 6 times. [36 sts]

Round 7: (5 sc, 1 sc inc) 6 times. [42 sts]

Round 8: (6 sc, 1 sc inc) 6 times. [48 sts]

Rounds 9–12: 1 sc in each st. [48 sts]

Round 13: BLO 1 sc inc in each st. [96 sts]

Rounds 14–19: 1 sc in each st. [96 sts]

HAT BAND

On Round 13 of the Hat: FLO reverse sc in each st with the color sea green, join to the 1st st, and fasten off.

Place the Hat on the Head and sew in place.

WINGS

Using the color ecru:

BASE OF THE WINGS

Round 1: 8 sc in MR.

Round 2: Ch 3 counts as a dc, [(1 dc, ch 2, 1 dc) in the next st, 1 dc] 4 times.

Do not fasten off.

FIRST PRIMARY WING

Step 1: Continuing from the Base, 2 sl sts to the 1st ch-2 sp.

Step 2: Ch 12, sl st to the next dc, ch-12, sl st to the next ch-2 sp, ch 1, turn.

Step 3: 12 sc around the 1st ch-12, sl st to the middle dc between the ch-2 sps, 12 sc around the 2nd ch-12 sp, ch 1, turn.

Step 4: 6 sc, 2 dc in the next st, ch 8, 2 dc in the 5th st (counting from the center dc), 6 sc, sl st into the ch-2 sp, ch 1, turn.

Step 5: 8 sc, 8 sc around ch-8 sp, 8 sc, sl st into ch-2 sp, ch 1, turn.

Insert the jewelry wire into this row:

Step 6: 2 hdc around the wire in each st, ch 1, turn.

Step 7: 3 sc along the base to the next ch-2 sp, sl st into the ch-2 sp.

SECOND PRIMARY WING

Repeat Steps 2–6 of the First Primary Wing. Fasten off.

Fig. 3

SECONDARY WING (MAKE 2)

Refer to the Secondary Wing pattern (page 22).

Attach each Secondary Wing to the Base by aligning the 1st row of the Wing to each of the ch-2 sps of the Base (*Fig. 3*).

Sew the Wings to the back of the Body.

STARFISH

Start with the color peace:

Round 1: 5 sc in a MR. [5 sts]

Round 2: 1 sc inc in each st, insert the mini hair elastic between one of your sts. (Follow the same technique of crocheting over jewelry wire in the Primary Wings.) [10 sts]

Round 3: [Ch 5, starting in the 2nd ch from the hook, 1 sl st, 1 sc, 1 hdc, 1 dc, skip 1 st, sl st into the next st] 5 times.

Fasten off. Wrap the mini elastic around the fairy's left hand.

CHAPTER 4

Bramble the Autumn Fairy

SKILL LEVEL: SPRINKLE

Bramble is the autumn fairy who fills the world with the colors of fall. Her bright orange wings shine in the sunlight, and she wears a belt decorated with maple leaves in every shade of the season. She loves jumping into piles of freshly fallen leaves that she's just finished coloring, celebrating the change of seasons with her cheerful laugh.

Finished Height:
- 9" (22.9cm)

Tools and Materials:
- US C/2 (2.75mm) and US B/1 (2.25mm) crochet hooks
- Two 6mm safety eyes
- Basic Craft Supplies (page 12)
- Basic Crochet Tools (page 11)

Yarn:
- YarnArt Jeans (Weight: #2 Fine)
    - Color 70 (Cocoa)—1 ball
    - Color 03 (Polar White)—1 ball
    - Color 84 (Mustard)—1 ball
    - Color 28 (Dark Gray)—1 ball
    - Color 53 (Black)—1 ball
    - Color 66 (Rosewood)—1 ball
    - Color 85 (Burnt Orange)—1 ball
    - Color 82 (Olive Green)—1 ball
    - Color 48 (Khaki)—1 ball

Pattern Notes:
- Follow the master fairy doll pattern (page 15) first before continuing with this pattern, using the following colors:
    - Legs—mustard and cocoa
    - Head/Arms—cocoa
        - When working the Arm, follow the master pattern up to Round 11.
    - Hair Wig—black
    - Body—polar white and mustard
- Rounds are joined and not crocheted in spirals. At the end of each round, join with a slip stitch in the first stitch of that round, then chain 1.
- Use a US C/2 (2.75mm) crochet hook unless otherwise stated.
- If instructed to cut a piece of yarn, use 36" (91.4cm) unless otherwise stated.

HAIR

Picking up from Round 19 of the Hair Wig, move on to Round 20. Round 20 will create Bramble's hairstyle. Continue with the same color (black):

Round 20: (Ch 1, sl st) in each st around.

Fasten off and leave a long tail for sewing the Hair to the Head.

Fig. 1

Fig. 2

HAIR BUN (MAKE 2)

Round 1: 8 sc in a MR.

Round 2: BLO 1 sc inc in each st. [16 sts]

Round 3: BLO (1 sc, 1 sc inc) 8 times. [24 sts]

Round 4: BLO 1 sc in each st. [24 sts]

Round 5: BLO (2 sc, 1 sc inc) 8 times. [32 sts]

Round 6: BLO 1 sc in each st. [32 sts]

Round 7. (Ch 1, sl st in the next st) 32 times (*Fig. 1*). [32 sts]

Do not fasten off, but continue working the following steps:

Step 1: Ch 1 and sl st into the front loop in Round 6.

Step 2: In the FLO of Round 6 *(ch 3, sl st in the next st)* 32 times, ch 1, and sl st into the front loop in Round 5.

Step 3: In the FLO of Round 5, repeat Step 2 from * to * 24 times.

Repeat from * to * in the FLO of Rounds 4, 3, then 2 (*Fig. 2*).

Fasten off and leave a long tail for sewing each Bun to the side of her Head. Stuff each Hair Bun lightly prior to sewing it onto the Head.

Sew the Hair Wig to the Head, and then sew the Buns to the Hair as shown.

ARM (Make 2)

Picking up from Round 10 of the Arm, move on to Round 11. Change to the color mustard at the end of Round 10.

Round 11: 1 sc in each st. [8 sts]

Round 12: BLO 1 sc in each st. [8 sts]

Rounds 13–16: Follow the master pattern to finish the sleeves on the Arm.

SLEEVE OF SHIRT

Using the color mustard: On the front loop of Round 12 on the Arm: Ch 4, 1 dc, in the same st as the ch, ch 1, [(1 dc, ch 1, 1 dc) in the same st, ch 1] 4 times and join to the top of the 1st ch-4 sp.

Fasten off and weave in the yarn inside the Arm.

SKIRT

Starting with the color dark gray:

Round 1: 1 sc in the FLO of Round 8 of the Body. [24 sts]

Round 2: (3 sc, 1 sc inc) 6 times. [30 sts]

Round 3: (4 sc, 1 sc inc) 6 times. [36 sts]

Round 4. 1 sc in each st. [36 sts]

Rounds 5–12: 1 sc in each st. [36 sts]

Fasten off.

Fig. 3

LEAVES

MAPLE LEAF (MAKE 2)

Make 1 using the color rosewood and 1 using the color khaki for the Belt.

Step 1: Ch 10, sl st into the 4th ch from the hook, sl st in the next ch.

Step 2: Ch 4, sl st in the 2nd ch from the hook, 1 sc, 1 hdc, skip 1 ch, (sl st in the next ch) 2 times.

Step 3: Ch 5, sl st in the 2nd ch from the hook, 1 sc, 2 hdc, skip 1 ch, sl st into the last ch.

Step 4: Ch 3, sl st in the 2nd ch from the hook, (sl st in the next ch) 2 times. Rotate the piece with the other side up and begin working along the opposite side of the foundation ch.

Step 5. Ch 1, 1 sc along the opposite side of the foundation ch.

Step 6: Ch 5, sl st into the 2nd ch from the hook, 1 sc, 2 hdc, skip 2 chs, sl st in the 1st ch of the foundation ch.

Fasten off and leave a long tail for sewing (*Fig. 3*).

SMALL LEAF (MAKE 2)

Make 1 using the color burnt orange and 1 using the color olive green for the Belt.

Step 1: Ch 6. Starting in the 2nd chain from the hook, 2 dc, 1 hdc, 1 sc, 1 sl st, ch 2.

Step 2: Working on the opposite side of the foundation ch, 1 sl st, 1 sc, 1 hdc, 1 dc, ch 1, and sl st into the 1st chain.

Fasten off and leave a tail for sewing.

BELT

Fig. 4

Using the color olive green, ch 80. Make an overhand knot in each end.

Attach the Leaves close to each other and layer them on top of one another, over 3 or 4 chs of the Belt (*Fig. 4*).

Double wrap the Belt around Bramble's waist with the Leaves at the front of her Skirt.

HAIR TIE

Using the color olive green, ch 35 and join to the 1st ch with a sl st. Fasten off.

Using the same leaf patterns, make 1 Maple Leaf with the color rosewood and 1 Small Leaf with the color khaki; however, cut a long piece of yarn and split the yarn in half. Use a US B/1 (2.25mm) crochet hook as you follow the pattern.

Attach the leaves close to each other, and layer them on top of one another over 3 or 4 chs of the wrap. Place it around one of the Hair Buns.

WINGS

BASE OF THE WINGS

Starting with the color black:

Round 1: 6 sc in a MR.

Round 2: 1 sc inc in each st. [12 sts]

Round 3: [2 sc, (1 sc, ch 2, 1 sc) in the same st] 4 times.

Fasten off.

PRIMARY WING (MAKE 2)

Fig. 5

Fig. 6

You will be crocheting in rows to create the Wings. Starting with the color burnt orange:

Row 1: Ch 5, starting in the 2nd ch from the hook, 4 sc, ch 1, turn. [4 sts]

Row 2: 1 sc inc, 3 sc, ch 1, turn. [5 sts]

Row 3: 4 sc, 1 sc inc, ch 1, turn. [6 sts]

Row 4: 1 sc inc, 5 sc, ch 1, turn. [7 sts]

Row 5: 6 sc, 1 sc inc, ch 1, turn. [8 sts]

Row 6: 1 sc inc, 7 sc, ch 1, turn. [9 sts]

Row 7: 9 sc, ch 1, turn. [9 sts]

Row 8: 1 sc inc, 8 sc, ch 1, turn. [10 sts]

Row 9: 1 sc inc, 9 sc, ch 1, turn. [11 sts]

Rows 10–11: 11 sc, ch 1, turn. [11 sts]

Row 12: 2 sc dec, 7 sc, ch 1, turn. [9 sts]

Row 13: 2 sc dec, 4 sc, 1 sc dec, ch 1, turn. [7 sts]

Row 14: 3 sc dec. [3 sts]

Fasten off.

Using the color black, attach to the bottom of the 1st ch of the foundation ch with a sl st. 4 sc across the bottom of the foundation ch. Insert the jewelry wire by attaching it with 1 sc. Sc around the jewelry wire edging on the wing to create a black outline when finished (*Fig. 5*).

Before fastening off, attach the Wing to the base with 4 sc from one corner of the Base to another corner.

Use the black yarn and long embroidered stitches to create veins in the Wings (*Fig. 6*).

Fig. 7

SECONDARY WING (MAKE 2)

Refer to the Secondary Wing pattern (page 22) and use the color black.

Attach each Secondary Wing from one corner ch-2 sp to the other corner (*Fig. 7*).

Sew the Wings to the back of the Body.

With the use of jewelry wire in the wings, you can pose them as you see fit!

CHAPTER 4

Merri the Winter Fairy

SKILL LEVEL: SPARKLE

Merri is the winter fairy who focuses on crafting each snowflake with pure winter magic. She camouflages into the flurries with her glistening snowflake wings and always dresses with just the right amount of gear so she can build snowmen at any given moment.

Finished Height:
- 9" (22.9cm)

Tools and Materials:
- US C/2 (2.75mm) crochet hook
- Two 6mm safety eyes
- Basic Craft Supplies (page 12)
- Basic Crochet Tools (page 11)

Yarn:
- YarnArt Jeans (Weight: #2 Fine)
    - Color 05 (Ecru)—1 ball
    - Color 73 (Peach)—1 ball
    - Color 49 (Pearl Gray)—1 ball
    - Color 46 (Light Gray)—1 ball
    - Color 03 (Polar White)—1 ball
    - Color 68 (Steel Blue)—1 ball
- YarnArt Jeans Soft Colors (Weight: #2 Fine)
    - Color 6213 (Variegated Blue)—1 ball

Pattern Notes:
- Follow the master fairy doll pattern (page 15) first before continuing with this pattern, using the following colors:
    - Legs—light gray and peach
    - Arms/Head—peach
    - Hair Wig—pearl gray
    - Body—polar white and peach
- Rounds are joined and not crocheted in spirals. At the end of each round, join with a slip stitch in the first stitch of that round, then chain 1.
- If instructed to cut a piece of yarn, use 36" (91.4cm) unless otherwise stated.

HAIR

Fig. 1

Picking up from Round 19 of the Hair Wig, move on to Round 20. Round 20 will create Merri's hairstyle. Continue with the same color (pearl gray):

Round 20:

- **Part 1**—(Ch 2, sl st) 2 times, 1 sc, 1 hdc, (ch 25, starting in the 2nd ch from the hook, 23 sl st along the ch, sc in next st) 3 times, these will form the three strands for the braid (*Fig. 1*).
- **Part 2**—2 hdc, 2 hdc in the next st, 2 dc, 1 tr, 2 tr in the next st, 6 tr, 2 dc, 2 hdc, 1 sc, 1 sl st, 1 sc, 1 hdc, 2 dc in the next st, 2 dc, 1 hdc, 1 sc, 1 sl st, which frames her face and parts her hair.
- **Part 3**—(Ch 2, sl st) 8 times, join.

Fasten off and sew the Hair to the Head.

Braid the three chains and tie a tiny bow with the color steel blue.

SWEATER

Fig. 2

Fig. 3

Using the color steel blue, crochet in rows:

Row 1: Ch 21, starting in the 2nd ch from the hook, 20 sc, ch 1, turn. [20 sts]

Row 2: 1 sc inc, 1 sc, ch 6, skip 4, 8 sc, ch 6, skip 4, 1 sc, 1 sc inc, ch 1, turn. [26 sts]

Row 3: 3 sc, 6 sc along the ch, 8 sc, 6 sc along the ch, 3 sc, ch 1, turn. [26 sts]

Row 4: 10 sc, 1 sc inc, 4 sc, 1 sc inc, 10 sc, ch 1, turn. [28 sts]

Row 5: 6 sc, 1 sc inc, 6 sc, 2 sc inc, 6 sc, 1 sc inc, 6 sc, ch 1, turn. [32 sts]

Row 6: 1 sc in each st, ch 1, turn. [32 sts]

Row 7: 1 sc inc, 7 sc, 1 sc inc, 14 sc, 1 sc inc, 7 sc, 1 sc inc, ch 1, turn. [36 sts]

Row 8: 1 sc in each st, ch 1, turn. [36 sts]

Row 9: (5 sc, 1 sc inc) 3 times, (1 sc inc, 5 sc) 3 times, ch 1, turn. [42 sts]

Row 10: 1 sc in each st, join with a sl st to the 1st st of the row (*Fig. 2*). [42 sts]

The remaining pattern for the Sweater will be done in rounds, and the V-shaped opening is at the back of the Sweater.

Rounds 11–14: 1 sc in each st. [42 sts]

The following round forms the pennants at the bottom of the sweater:

Round 15: *6 sc, ch 1, turn, 3 sc dec, ch 1, turn, 1 sc dec, 1 sc, ch 1, turn, 1 sc dec for the point, ch 1, turn, 4 sl sts down the side of the pennant, sl st to next st in Round 15.* Start the next pennant in the last sl st. Repeat the steps from * to * 6 more times (*Fig. 3*).

Fasten off.

Fig. 4

RIGHT SLEEVE

For the Sleeves, work in spiral rounds.

Round 1: Start in the back corner of the armhole with a sl st, 5 sc across the top of the armhole, 9 sl st across the bottom of the armhole, do not join (*Fig. 4*). Keep the sl st loose.

Rounds 2–3: 5 sc, 9 sl st. [14 sts]

Rounds 3–15: 1 sc in each st. [14 sts]

Fasten off and weave in the tail.

LEFT SLEEVE

Round 1: Start in the back corner of the armhole with a sl st, 9 sl st across the bottom of the armhole, 5 sc across the top of the armhole, do not join. Keep the sl st loose.

Rounds 2–3: 5 sc, 9 sl st. [14 sts]

Rounds 3–15: 1 sc in each st. [14 sts]

Fasten off and weave in the tail.

SNOW PANTS

Start with the color ecru:

PANT LEG (MAKE 2)

Round 1: Ch 16 and join to the 1st ch with a sl st. [16 sts]

Round 2: 1 sc in each ch. [16 sts]

Round 3: 1 sc in each st. [16 sts]

Round 4: (3 sc, 1 sc inc) 4 times. [20 sts]

Rounds 5–14: 1 sc in each st. [20 sts]

Fasten off the 1st Leg, but do not fasten off the 2nd Leg. Once you have made the 2nd Leg, ch 2 and join it to the 1st Leg with a sc st. This will be the start of the rounds going forward.

Round 15: Ch 1, 19 sc, 2 sc in the ch, 20 sc, 2 sc in opposite side of the ch, join. [44 sts]

Rounds 16–18: 1 sc in each st. [44 sts]

Round 19: (9 sc, 1 sc dec) 4 times. [40 sts]

Round 20: 1 sc in each st. [40 sts]

Round 21: (8 sc, 1 sc dec) 4 times. [36 sts]

Rounds 22–23: 1 st in each st. [36 sts]

Round 24: (7 sc, 1 sc dec) 4 times [32 sts]

Fasten off and weave in the tail.

FRONT OF SNOW PANTS

Fig. 5

The Front of the Snow Pants is worked in rows. To center it, fold the Pants in half to find where to center your stitches, and place a marker.

Row 1: Begin 5 sts before the marker, 10 sc, ch 1, turn. [10 sts]

Rows 2–5: 1 sc in each st, ch 1, turn. [10 sts]

Row 6: 1 sc in each st, do not turn. Ch 12 and cross the ch over to the center back of the Pants with a sl st to join. With the back of the Pants facing you, create 2 sl sts on the Pants and ch 12, cross the ch over to the opposite front corner of the Pants, and connect with a sl st (*Fig. 5*).

Fasten off.

Place the Snow Pants on the Body. Place the Sweater on the Body.

JACKET VEST

Using the color ecru, crochet in rows:

Row 1: Ch 21, starting in the 2nd ch from the hook, 20 hdc in each ch, ch 1, turn.

The rest of the Jacket Vest is worked in the BLO unless stated otherwise.

Row 2: BLO 1 hdc inc, ch 10, skip 5 sts, 1 hdc inc, 6 hdc, hdc inc, ch 10, skip 5, 1 hdc inc in last st. [34 sts]

Row 3: 2 hdc, 10 hdc around the ch, 10 hdc, 10 hdc around the 2nd ch, 2 hdc. [34 sts]

Rows 4–7: 1 hdc in each st, ch 1, turn.

Row 8: 1 hdc in each st, do not turn.

EDGING

11 sc, (1 sc, ch 1, 1 sc) in the corner, 20 sc across the collar, (1 sc, ch 1, 1 sc) in the corner, 11 sc, ch 1, 34 sc across, ch 1, and join. Fasten off and weave in the yarn.

Place the Jacket Vest on the Body.

HAT

Using the variegated blue yarn, start with the ribbed edge of the hat.

RIBBING

Row 1: Ch 5, starting in the 2nd ch from the hook, 4 sc, ch 1, turn. [4 sts]

Rows 2–46: BLO 1 sc in each st, ch 1, turn. [4 sts]

Join Row 1 to Row 46 with a sl st through the BLO of Row 46 and the FLO of Row 1.

Continue to work in the round. Join with a sl st to the 1st st at the end of each round, then ch 1.

BEANIE

Round 1: 1 sc into the top of each row of the ribbed edge. [46 sts]

Rounds 2–14: 1 sc in each st. [46 sts]

Round 15: (2 sc, 1 sc dec) 11 times, 2 sc. [35 sts]

Fasten off and leave a tail for sewing.

Turn the piece inside out. Using a wide running stitch, sew through the last round and pull tight to close the top of the Hat.

Fasten off and weave in the yarn. Turn the piece right side out.

Make a small pom-pom and sew it at the top of the Hat (optional).

Sew the Hat to the Head.

MITTEN (Make 2)

Using the variegated blue yarn to match the Hat:

RIGHT HAND

Round 1: 6 sc in a MR. [6 sts]

Round 2: 1 sc inc in each st. [12 sts]

Round 3: 1 sc in each st. [12 sts]

Round 4: (2 sc, 1 sc dec) 3 times. [9 sts]

Round 5: 2 sc, 1 Bo in next st, 6 sc. [9 sts]

Round 6: 1 sc in each st. [9 sts]

Round 7: (Sl st, ch 1) 9 times, ch 13, and sl st into the same st.

Fasten off.

LEFT HAND

Round 1: 6 sc in a MR. [6 sts]

Round 2: 1 sc inc in each st. [12 sts]

Round 3: 1 sc in each st. [12 sts]

Round 4: (2 sc, 1 sc dec) 3 times. [9 sts]

Round 5: 6 sc, 1 Bo st in next st, 2 sc. [9 sts]

Round 6: 1 sc in each st. [9 sts]

Round 7: (Sl st, ch 1) 9 times, ch 13, and sl st into the same st.

Fasten off. Hang the Mittens from her hands.

SCARF

Using the variegated blue yarn to match the Hat and Mittens, crochet in rows:

Row 1: Ch 6, starting in the 2nd ch from the hook, (1 sc, 1 dc) 2 times, 1 sc, ch 2, turn. [5 sts]

Row 2: The ch 2 at the end of Row 1 counts as your 1st dc, 1 sc in next st, 1 dc, 1 sc, 1 dc, ch 1, turn. [5 sts]

Row 3: 1 sc in the same st as ch 1, 1 dc, 1 sc, 1 dc, 1 sc, ch 2, turn. [5 sts]

Rows 4–40: Repeat Rows 2 and 3 alternately. [5 sts]

Fasten off. If desired, add tassels to the ends of the Scarf by tying small pieces of yarn to each st.

WINGS

Using the color polar white:

Fig. 6

Fig. 7

PRIMARY WING (MAKE 2)

Round 1: 6 sc in MR. [6 sts]

Round 2: 1 sc inc in each st. [12 sts]

Round 3: Ch 3, 1 dc, ch 3, (2 dc, ch 3) 5 times, join to the top of the 1st ch-3 sp (*Fig. 6*). (First ch-3 sp represents the first dc). [30 sts]

Round 4: [2 sc, (2 dc, ch 3, 2 dc) in ch-3 sp], 6 times. [54 sts]

Round 5: Ch 3, *2 dc, 1 tr, (2 tr, ch 3, 2 tr) in ch-3 sp, 1 tr, 2 dc*, repeat from * to * 4 more times, 2 dc, 1 tr, (2 tr, ch 3, 2 tr) in ch-3 sp, 1 tr, 1 dc, join (*Fig. 7*). [78 sts]

Insert jewelry wire on this round:

Round 6. 1 sc in each st, 3 sc in each ch-3 sp, join.

Fasten off and weave in the yarn.

ASSEMBLY

These Wings do not use a Base to anchor to. In addition, Merri does not have a set of Secondary Wings.

Step 1: Using the Primary Wings, with right sides together, overlap two points of the snowflake so they align and sew them together.

Step 2: Sew the Wings to the back of the Jacket Vest.

Wrap the Scarf around the neck.

CHAPTER 4

Rosalie the Spring Fairy

SKILL LEVEL: SPRINKLE

Rosalie is the fairy in charge of bringing spring to life each year. With her petal-pink wings and a simple crown of flower buds, she travels through the fields and forests, tapping on plants to let them know it's time to grow and bloom. Wherever she goes, colors return and the world begins to wake up again. To Rosalie, spring isn't just another part of the year—it's a fresh start and a time to celebrate new beginnings.

Finished Height:
- 9" (22.9cm)

Tools and Materials:
- US C/2 (2.75mm) crochet hook
- Two 6mm safety eyes
- Basic Craft Supplies (page 12)
- Basic Crochet Tools (page 11)

Yarn:
- YarnArt Jeans (Weight: #2 Fine)
    - Color 73 (Peach)—1 ball
    - Color 03 (Polar White)—1 ball
    - Color 18 (Light Pink)—1 ball
    - Color 19 (Lavender)—1 ball
    - Color 11 (Pastel Green)—1 ball
    - Color 70 (Cocoa)—1 ball

Pattern Notes:
- Follow the master fairy doll pattern (page 15) first before continuing with this pattern, using the following colors:
    - Legs—pastel green and peach
    - Head/Arms—peach
        - When working the Arm, follow the master pattern up to Round 12.
    - Hair Wig—cocoa
    - Body—polar white and pastel green
- Rounds are joined and not crocheted in spirals. At the end of each round, join with a slip stitch in the first stitch of that round, then chain 1.
- If instructed to cut a piece of yarn, use 36" (91.4cm) unless otherwise stated.

ARM (Make 2)

Picking up from Round 11 of the Arm, move on to Round 12. Change to the color pastel green at the end of Round 11.

Rounds 12–13: BLO 1 sc in each st. [8 sts]

Rounds 14–16: Follow the master pattern to finish the sleeves on the Arm.

Once the Arm is complete, on the FLO of Rounds 12 and 13, sl st into each st to create an edged sleeve.

HAIR

Picking up from Round 19 of the Hair Wig, move on to Round 20. Round 20 will create Rosalie's hairstyle. Continue with the same color (cocoa):

Round 20: (Ch 1, 1 sl st) 15 times, 1 sc, 1 hdc, 2 dc in same st, 2 tr, 2 tr in same st, 1 dc, 1 hdc, 1 sc, 1 sl st, 2 hdc, 1 dc, 2 dc in the same st, 1 hdc, 1 sc, 1 sl st, (ch 1, 1 sl st) 11 times.

Fasten off and leave a long tail for sewing the Hair to the Head. Sew to the Head.

Fig. 1

HAIR BUN (MAKE 2)

Starting with the color cocoa:

Round 1: 6 sc in a MR. [6 sts]

Round 2: [Ch 10, (FLO 2 sc in each ch, sl st to the next st)] 6 times (*Fig. 1*).

Fasten off and leave a long tail for sewing each Bun to the top of her Head. Sew each Hair Bun between Rounds 6–8 of the Hair Wig.

HEADBAND

Using the color pastel green: Ch 13, beginning in the 3rd ch from the hook, *1 dc, 2 dc in the next st, 1 dc, ch 2 and sl st into the same ch*, sl st into the next ch, ch 1, repeat from * to * again, sl st into the next ch, ch 1, repeat from * to * once more to the end of the ch.

ROSE (MAKE 2)

Using the color lavender: Ch 13, beginning in the 3rd ch from the hook, *1 dc, 2 dc in the next st, 1 dc, ch 2 and sl st into the same ch*, sl st into the next ch, ch 1, repeat from * to * again, sl st into the next ch, ch 1, repeat from * to * once more to the end of the ch.

Fasten off. Curl the foundation ch to form a bud and sew each Rose in between the leaves on the Headband.

SKIRT

Fig. 2

Starting with the color lavender:

Round 1: In the FLO of Round 8 of the Body, (1 sc, ch 3, skip 3 sts) 6 times. [24 sts]

Round 2: (1 sc, 3 sc in ch-3 sp) 6 times. [24 sts]

Round 3: (1 sc, 1 sc inc) 12 times. [36 sts]

Rounds 4–14: 1 sc in each st. [36 sts]

Round 15: BLO 1 sc in each st. [36 sts]

Round 16: Ch 1, (skip 2, 5 dc in same st) 11 times, skip 2, sl st in the beginning of ch 1 (*Fig. 2*).

Fasten off and weave in the yarn.

LEAVES

Fig. 3

LARGE LEAF (MAKE 6)

Using the color pastel green: Ch 11, starting in the 2nd chain from the hook, 2 tr, 2 dc, 2 hdc, 2 sc, 1 sl st, ch 2. Rotate the piece to work along the opposite side of the foundation ch, 1 sl st, 2 sc, 2 hdc, 2 dc, 2 tr, ch 1, join with a sl st in the beginning ch.

Fasten off and leave a tail for sewing (*Fig. 3*).

SMALL LEAF (MAKE 6)

Using the color pastel green: Ch 6, starting in the 2nd chain from the hook, 2 dc, 1 hdc, 1 sc, 1 sl st, ch 2. Rotate the piece to work along the opposite side of the foundation ch, 1 sl st, 1 sc, 1 hdc, 1 dc, ch 1, and sl st into the 1st chain.

Fasten off and leave a tail for sewing (*Fig. 3*).

ASSEMBLY

Sew each Large Leaf above the FLO on Round 8 of the Body where each ch-3 sp is located (*Fig. 4*).

Sew each Small Leaf above and between each Large Leaf.

Using the color pastel purple, embroider a small flower to the front of the Dress.

Fig. 4

WINGS

Using the color pastel pink:

Fig. 5

Fig. 6

BASE OF THE WINGS

Round 1: Ch 3, 2 dc into the 3rd ch from the hook, ch 2, (3 dc into the 3rd ch from the hook, ch 2) 3 times, join to the top of the 1st ch-3 sp (*Fig. 5*).

Round 2: [3 sc, (1 sc, ch 2, 1 sc in the ch-2 sp)] 4 times, join to the 1st sc.

Fasten off and weave in the yarn (*Fig. 6*).

Fig. 7

Fig. 8

Fig. 9

PRIMARY WING (MAKE 2)

You will be crocheting in rows to create the Primary Wings.

Row 1: Ch 10, starting in the 2nd ch from the hook, 1 sc inc, 7 sc, 4 sc in the last ch, rotate the piece to work along the opposite side of the foundation ch, 7 sc, 1 sc inc, do not join the round, ch 1, turn (*Fig. 7*). [22 sts]

Row 2: 9 sc, 4 sc inc, 9 sc, ch 1, turn. [26 sts]

Row 3: 3 sc, ch 8, skip 4 sts, 3 sc, 1 sc inc, 4 sc, 1 sc inc, 3 sc, ch 8, skip 4 sts, 3 sc, ch 1, turn. [20 sts, and 2 ch-8 sp]

Row 4: 3 sc, 9 sc around the ch-8 sp, 4 sc, ch 14, skip 6 sts, 4 sc, 9 sc around ch-8 sp, 3 sc, ch 1, turn (*Fig. 8*).

Insert the jewelry wire on this row:

Row 5: 16 sc, 16 sc over the ch-14 sp and wire held together, 16 sc, ch 1, turn.

Row 6: (Skip 2 sts, 5 dc in the same st, skip 2 sts, sl st) 8 times.

Fasten off and leave a long tail for sewing (*Fig. 9*).

SECONDARY WING (MAKE 2)

Refer to the Secondary Wing pattern (page 22).

Fig. 10

ASSEMBLY

Attach each Wing to the Base. Align ch-2 sps of the base with the 1st and last st of Row 6, and join with 5 sc (*Fig. 10*). Sew the Base to the back of the fairy.

Place the Headband on the Head.

CHAPTER 4

Unicorn Friends

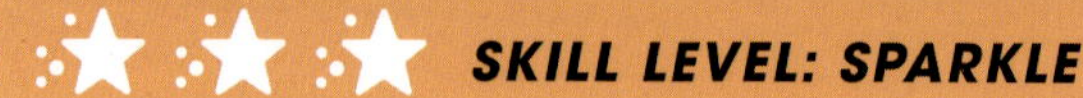

SKILL LEVEL: SPARKLE

In the hidden meadows of the fairy realm, the unicorns graze beneath the sky, each one bound to a season and its fairy guardian. Together, the unicorns and their fairy friends keep the balance of the seasons—painting the year with color and life.

Finished Height:

- 6" (15.2cm)

Tools and Materials:

- US C/2 (2.75mm) crochet hook
- Two 6mm safety eyes
- Basic Craft Supplies (page 12)
- Basic Crochet Tools (page 11)

Yarn:

- YarnArt Jeans (Weight: #2 Fine)
    - Color 73 (Peach)—1 ball
    - Color 77 (Orange)—1 ball
    - Color 85 (Burnt Orange)—1 ball
    - Color 11 (Pastel Green)—1 ball (*optional*)
    - Color 86 (Light Yellow)—1 ball
    - Color 35 (Sunflower)—1 ball

Pattern Notes:

- Rounds are joined and not crocheted in spirals. At the end of each round, join with a slip stitch in the first stitch of that round, then chain 1.
- If instructed to cut a piece of yarn, use 36" (91.4cm) unless otherwise stated.

HEAD

Fig. 1

Using the color light yellow, the pattern will start at the back of the head:

Round 1: 6 sc in a MR. [6 sts]

Round 2: 6 sc inc. [12 sts]

Round 3: (1 sc, 1 sc inc) 6 times. [18 sts]

Round 4: (2 sc, 1 sc inc) 6 times. [24 sts]

Round 5: (3 sc, 1 sc inc) 6 times. [30 sts]

Round 6: (4 sc, 1 sc inc) 6 times. [36 sts]

Rounds 7–11: 1 sc in each st. [36 sts]

Place the eyes between Rounds 8 and 9, about 13 sts apart and centered on the face. Begin to stuff the Head.

Round 12: Ch 9, skip the next 13 sts, 23 sc, and join to the 1st ch (*Fig. 1*). [32 sts]

Round 13: 1 sc in each st (working 9 sc over the ch-9 sp to begin forming the nose and face). [32 sts]

Rounds 14–19: 1 sc in each st, changing to the color peach at the end of Round 19, and insert the eyes on Round 15. [32 sts]

Round 20: (2 sc, 1 sc dec) 8 times. [24 sts]

Round 21: (1 sc, 1 sc dec) 8 times. [16 sts]

Round 22: (2 sc, 1 sc dec) 4 times. [12 sts]

Round 23: 6 sc dec. [6 sts]

Fasten off and weave in the yarn.

Fig. 2

NECK

Continuing with the color light yellow, join to the left corner of the Head to begin forming the Neck:

Round 1: 12 sc, 1 sc dec in the opposite corner, 8 sc along the ch from the Head, 1 sc dec in the corner you started from (*Fig. 2*). [22 sts]

Round 2: 1 sc in each st. [22 sts]

Round 3: 12 sc, 1 sc dec, 6 sc, 1 sc dec. [20 sts]

Rounds 4–8: 1 sc in each st. [20 sts]

BODY

Fig. 3

Continuing the rounds from the Neck:

Round 9: 7 sc, ch 15, beginning in the 2nd ch on the hook, 1 sc inc, 13 sc, 1 sc into the next st on the Neck, 12 sc (*Fig. 3*). [35 sts]

Round 10: 6 sc, 1 sc dec (with 1 loop from the Neck and 1 loop from the 1st ch of Round 9), 12 sc, rotate piece to work along the opposite side of the foundation ch from Round 9, 1 sc inc in the last ch of the foundation ch, 14 sc, 1 sc dec (in the last ch and the next st of Round 9), 12 sc. [48 sts]

Round 11: 19 sc, 1 sc inc, 3 sc, 1 sc inc, 24 sc. [50 sts]

Round 12: 19 sc, 6 sc inc, 25 sc. [56 sts]

Round 13: 21 sc, 1 sc inc, 6 sc, 1 sc inc, 27 sc. [58 sts]

Rounds 14–25: 1 sc in each st. [58 sts]

This round will begin to form the openings for the Legs:

Round 26: (6 sc, 1 sc dec) 7 times, 2 sc. [51 sts]

Round 27: (3 sc, 1 sc dec) 10 times, 1 sc. [41 sts]

Round 28: (Ch 5, skip 7 sts, 3 sc) 4 times and join to the 1st ch. [32 sts]

Round 29: (2 sc, 1 sc dec) 8 times. [24 sts]

Round 30: (1 sc, 1 sc dec) 8 times. [16 sts]

Round 31: (2 sc, 1 sc dec) 4 times. [12 sts]

Round 32: 6 sc dec. [6 sts]

Fasten off and weave in the yarn.

LEG (Make 4)

Fig. 4

Fig. 5

Continuing with the color light yellow, join to the right corner of one of the Body openings with a sl st:

Round 1: (1 sc, 1 sc inc) 6 times (*Figs. 4 and 5*). [18 sts]

Rounds 2–10: 1 sc in each st, changing to the color peach at the end of Round 10. [18 sts]

Rounds 11–12: 1 sc in each st. [18 sts]

Round 13: BLO (1 sc, 1 sc dec) 6 times. [12 sts]

Round 14: 6 sc dec. [6 sts]

Fasten off and weave in the yarn.

EAR (Make 2)

Starting with the color light yellow:

Round 1: 6 sc in a MR. [6 sts]

Round 2: 6 sc inc. [12 sts]

Round 3: (1 sc, 1 sc dec) 3 times. [9 sts]

Round 4: (2 sc, 1 sc inc) 3 times. [12 sts]

Round 5: (3 sc, 1 sc inc) 3 times. [15 sts]

Rounds 6–7: 1 sc in each st. [15 sts]

Round 8: (3 sc, 1 sc dec) 3 times. [12 sts]

Fasten off and weave in the yarn. Do not stuff the edges but fold it, and whipstitch the Ear together before sewing it to the Head between Rounds 7–9.

HORN

Using the color sunflower:

Round 1: 4 sc in a MR. [4 sts]

Round 2: 1 sc in each st. [4 sts]

Round 3: (1 sc, 1 sc inc) 2 times. [6 sts]

Round 4: 1 sc in each st. [6 sts]

Round 5: (1 sc, 1 inc) 3 times. [9 sts]

Rounds 6–7: 1 sc in each st. [9 sts]

Fasten off. Lightly stuff the Horn before sewing it to the center of the forehead.

Fig. 6

Fig. 7

MANE (Make 3)

Make 2 using the color burnt orange and 1 using the color orange:

- Ch 28, starting in the 2nd ch from the hook, 1 sc, [ch 10, starting in the 2nd ch from the hook (1 sc inc, 1 sc) 4 times, 1 sc inc in the last ch of the ch-10 sp, 1 sc into the next 2 ch of the foundation ch] 13 times (*Fig. 6*).
- Ch 5, starting in the 2nd ch from the hook, 4 sc inc, and sl st into the last ch of the foundation ch.

Sew the short ch-5 sp to the top of the Head next to the Horn, and sew the rest of the Mane down the Neck (*Fig. 7*).

TAIL

Starting with the color burnt orange:

- 6 sc in a MR. [6 sts]
- [Ch 25, starting in the 2nd ch from the hook, (1 sc inc, 1 sc) 11 times, 1 inc, sl st into the last ch of the foundation ch, sl st in the sc of the last round] 6 times.

Fasten off and weave in the yarn. Sew the Tail at the back of the Body.

SADDLE

This accessory is optional.

Starting with the color pastel green:

Round 1: Ch 14, starting in the 2nd ch from the hook, 1 sc inc, 11 sc, 2 sc inc in the last ch, rotate the piece to work along the opposite side of the foundation ch, 11 sc, 1 sc inc. [30 sts]

Round 2: 1 sc, 1 sc inc, 11 sc, 1 sc inc, 2 sc, 1 sc inc, 11 sc, 1 sc inc, 1 sc. [34 sts]

Round 3: 1 sc, 1 sc inc, 13 sc, 1 sc inc, 2 sc, 1 sc inc, 13 sc, 1 sc inc, 1 sc. [38 sts]

Round 4: 6 sc, 1 hdc, 5 dc, 1 hdc, 12 sc, 1 hdc, 5 dc, 1 hdc, 6 sc. [38 sts]

Ch 30, then cut the yarn and leave a long tail for sewing.

Place the Saddle on the back and sew the end of the ch to the opposite side of the Saddle to form a strap.

Fasten off and weave in the yarn.

Chapter 5

Woodland Fairies and Their Toad Friends

The woodland fairies and their toad friends are at the heart of every forest, caring for each mushroom, log, and tree to keep nature full of life. Tilly tends to each mushroom, from tiny button mushrooms to towering toadstools, while Hazel watches over the forest trees and keeps an eye on the wildlife that calls the forest home. Together with their toad companions, they make the woodlands an enchanted place to explore.

CHAPTER 5

Tilly the Mushroom Fairy

SKILL LEVEL: SPARKLE

Tilly is the keeper of the forest's mushrooms, tending to every cap and stem with care and a splash of morning dew. She works side by side with her toad friends, who help her water the tiniest sprouts. Cheerful and curious, Tilly believes every mushroom has its own story, and she knows them all by name.

Finished Height:
- 9" (22.9cm)

Tools and Materials:
- US C/2 (2.75mm) crochet hook
- Two 6mm safety eyes
- Basic Craft Supplies (page 12)
- Basic Crochet Tools (page 11)

Yarn:
- YarnArt Jeans (Weight: #2 Fine)
    - Color 73 (Peach)—1 ball
    - Color 03 (Polar White)—1 ball
    - Color 07 (Tan)—1 ball
    - Color 70 (Cocoa)—1 ball
    - Color 48 (Khaki)—1 ball
    - Color 51 (Cherry)—1 ball
    - Color 05 (Ecru)—1 ball
    - Color 65 (Rose)—1 ball
    - Color 29 (Pistachio)—1 ball

Pattern Notes:
- Follow the master fairy doll pattern (page 15) first before continuing with this pattern, using the following colors:
    - Legs—cocoa and peach
    - Arms—peach and tan
    - Head—peach
    - Hair Wig—cocoa
    - Body—polar white and tan
- Rounds are joined and not crocheted in spirals. At the end of each round, join with a slip stitch in the first stitch of that round, then chain 1.
- If instructed to cut a piece of yarn, use 36" (91.4cm) unless otherwise stated.

HAIR

Fig. 1

Picking up from Round 19 of the Hair Wig, move on to Round 20. Round 20 will create Tilly's hairstyle. Continue with the same color (cocoa):

Round 20:

- **Part 1**—19 sl st.
- **Part 2**—*1 sc, ch 4, starting in the 2nd ch from the hook, 1 sl st, 2 sc, sl st into the same sc as the last sc*, repeat from * to * 4 more times.
- **Part 3**—20 sl st, join.

Sew the Hair to her Head, with the bangs in the center front of her face (*Fig. 1*).

Fig. 2

PIGTAIL (MAKE 2)

Continue with the color cocoa:

Round 1: 6 sc in MR. [6 sts]

Round 2: [Ch 21, starting in the 2nd ch from the hook, 2 sc in each ch to the 1st ch, sl st into the next st] 5 times (*Fig. 2*). [40 sts]

Sew each Pigtail to the side of the Head between Rounds 10–12 of the Wig.

SHORTS

Starting with the color dark brown:

RIGHT PANT LEG

Round 1: Ch 20, sl st in the 1st ch to form a ring, ch 1, 20 sc around the ch. [20 sts]

Round 2: (3 sc, 1 sc inc) 5 times. [25 sts]

Rounds 3–4: 1 sc in each st. [25 sts]

Fasten off and weave in the yarn.

LEFT PANT LEG

Repeat Rounds 1–4 of the Right Pant Leg to make the Left Pant Leg. Round 5 will join both Pant Legs together.

Round 5: Sl st in the Right Pant Leg, ch 1, join with 1 sc to the Left Pant Leg, 24 sc around, 1 sc in the ch, 25 sc around the Right Pant Leg, 1 sc in the opposite side of the ch, join. [52 sts]

Each round will now begin from this point.

Fig. 3

Round 6: 1 sc in each st. [52 sts]

Round 7: (11 sc, 1 sc dec) 4 times. [48 sts]

Round 8: (6 sc, 1 sc dec) 6 times. [42 sts]

Round 9: (4 sc, 1 sc dec) 7 times. [35 sts]

Rounds 10–13: 1 sc in each st. [35 sts]

This round will create the belt loops on the Shorts:

Round 14:

- **Step 1**—(4 sc, 1 sc into Round 13) 3 times.
- **Step 2**—(6 sc, 1 sc into Round 13), which will be the front of the Shorts.
- **Step 3**—(4 sc, 1 sc into Round 13) 2 times.
- **Step 4**—2 sc.

Fasten off and weave in the yarn.

BELT

Using the color khaki: Ch 56 and fasten off each end with an overhand knot.

Thread the Belt through the belt loops of the Shorts (*Fig. 3*). Place the Shorts on the Body.

MUSHROOM HAT

Starting with the color rose:

Round 1: 8 sc in MR. [8 sts]

Round 2: 1 sc inc in each st. [16 sts]

Round 3: (1 sc, 1 sc inc) 8 times. [24 sts]

Round 4: (2 sc, 1 sc inc) 8 times. [32 sts]

Round 5: (3 sc, 1 sc inc) 8 times. [40 sts]

Rounds 6–7: 1 sc in each st. [40 sts]

Round 8: (4 sc, 1 sc inc) 8 times. [48 sts]

Rounds 9–10: 1 sc in each st. [48 sts]

Round 11: (5 sc, 1 sc inc) 8 times. [56 sts]

Rounds 12–13: 1 sc in each st. [56 sts]

Round 14: BLO 1 reverse sc in each st. Do not fasten off but continue to create the chin strap. [56 sts]

Ch 28 and join to the opposite side of the Hat with a sl st. Fasten off and weave in the yarn.

LARGE SPOT (MAKE 4)

Using the color ecru:

Round 1: 6 sc in MR. [6 sts]

Round 2: 1 sc inc in each st. [12 sts]

SMALL SPOT (MAKE 5)

Using the color ecru: Work Round 1 of the Large Spot and fasten off.

ASSEMBLY

Sew the Large and Small Spots at random locations on top of the Mushroom Hat.

VEST

The Vest is made to allow the Wings to go through the back. Using the color pistachio, crochet in rows:

Row 1: Ch 21, starting in the 2nd ch from the hook, 1 sc in each st, ch 1, turn. [20 sts]

Row 2: 1 hdc inc, 18 sc, 1 hdc inc, ch 1, turn. [22 sts]

RIGHT FRONT

Fig. 4

Continuing the rows from the Vest:

Row 3: BLO 5 sc, ch 1, turn (*Fig. 4*). [5 sts]

Rows 4–15: 1 sc in each st, ch 1, turn. [5 sts]

Fasten off and weave in the yarn.

LEFT FRONT

Fig. 5

Continuing the rows from the Vest:

Row 3: Sl st into the 5th st from the end of Row 2, 1 sc in the same st, 4 sc, ch 1, turn (*Fig. 5*). [5 sts]

Rows 4–15: 1 sc in each st, ch 1, turn. [5 sts]

Fasten off and weave in the yarn.

MIDDLE OF THE BACK

Continuing the rows from the Vest:

Row 3: Make a sl st into st 10 from Row 2, 1 sc in the same st, 4 sc, ch 1, turn. [5 sts]

Rows 4–15: 1 sc in each st, ch 1, turn. [5 sts]

Fasten off.

BOTTOM OF THE VEST

Fig. 6

Row 1: Ch 23, starting in the 2nd ch from the hook, 1 sc in each st, ch 1, turn. [22 sts]

Rows 2–3: 1 sc in each st, ch 1, turn. [22 sts]

Fasten off and weave in the yarn.

Sew the Right Front and the Left Front to the Bottom. Sew the back of the Vest, centered on the Bottom of the Vest (*Fig. 6*).

FINISHING

Fig. 7

Once joined, create an edge around the entire Vest:

Starting on the top-left corner of the Vest: 17 sc down the left side, (1 sc, ch 1, 1 sc) in the corner, (1 sc, ch 2) in each st across the bottom, (1 sc, ch 1, 1 sc) in the corner, 17 sc up the right side (*Fig. 7*). Fasten off.

WINGS

BASE OF THE WINGS

Starting with the color rose:

Round 1: Ch 4 and join with a sl st to the 1st ch to form a ring.

Round 2: Ch 4, this will count as your 1st dc, 2 dc in the ring, ch 2, (3 dc in the ring, ch 2) 3 more times, sl st to the top of the ch-4 sp, ch 1. [12 sts, and 4 ch-2 sp]

Round 3: 1 sc in the same st, 2 sc, (1 sc, ch 1, 1 sc) in the ch-2 sp, *3 sc, (1 sc, ch 1, 1 sc) in the ch-2 sp*, repeat from * to * 2 more times, changing the color to ecru and joining to the 1st sc, ch 1. [20 sts, and 4 ch-1 sp]

Round 4: [4 sc, (1sc, ch 1, 1 sc)] 4 times, join to the 1st sc. [24 sts, and 4 ch-1 sp]

Fasten off.

PRIMARY WING (MAKE 2)

Fig. 8

You will be creating a swirl pattern for the Wings, using the colors rose and ecru. Starting with the color rose:

Step 1: Ch 4 and join with a sl st to the 1st ch to form a ring, 1 sc into the ring, 5 hdc, changing the color to ecru. Do not cut off the rose yarn. Using the color ecru, 6 hdc around the ring.

Step 2: Continuing with the color ecru, 1 hdc inc into the 1st sc from Step 1, 5 hdc inc. Drop the ecru and pick up the color rose again.

Step 3: 10 hdc inc, (2 hdc, 1 hdc inc) 3 times. Drop the rose and pick up the color ecru again.

Step 4: 4 hdc inc, (2 hdc, 1 hdc inc) 8 times. Drop the ecru and pick up the color rose again.

Step 5: (2 hdc, 1 hdc inc) 2 times, 2 sc. Fasten off the color rose. Pick up the color ecru again.

Step 6: 2 hdc, 8 sc. Do not fasten off (*Fig. 8*).

Step 7: Insert the wire on this step. 1 sc around the wire and each st of the Wing.

Fasten off and weave in the yarn.

Sew the Primary Wings to each side of the Base.

SECONDARY WING (MAKE 2)

Refer to the Secondary Wing pattern (page 22) and use the color rose.

Attach each Secondary Wing to the Base by aligning the 1st row of each of the ch-2 sp of the Base.

Sew the Wings to the back of the Body. Place the Vest on the doll and insert the Wings through the back of the Vest.

Using the color rose, cut two 3" (7.6cm) pieces of yarn. Use them to tie the Vest together at the top.

MUSHROOM (Make 2)

CAP

Starting with the color cherry:

Round 1: 6 sc in a MR. [6 sts]

Round 2: 1 sc inc in each st. [12 sts]

Round 3: (1 sc, 1 sc inc) 3 times. [18 sts]

Round 4: BLO 1 sc in each st. [18 sts]

Round 5: BLO 9 sc dec. [9 sts]

Round 6: (1 sc, 1 sc dec) 3 times. [6 sts]

Fasten off and weave in the yarn.

STEM

Fig. 9

Using the color ecru:

Round 1: 6 sc in a MR. [6 sts]

Round 2: (1 sc, 1 sc inc) 3 times. [9 sts]

Round 3: BLO 1 sc in each st. [9 sts]

Round 4: (1 sc, 1 sc dec) 3 times. [6 sts]

Rounds 5–6: 1 sc in each st. [6 sts]

Fasten off and leave a long tail for sewing.

Sew the Cap to the Stem, and make small stitches on the Cap to create the spots (*Fig. 9*).

BAG

Using the color khaki:

Round 1: Ch 9, starting in the 2nd ch from the hook, 1 sc inc, 6 sc, 3 sc in the last ch, rotate the piece to work along the opposite side of the foundation ch, 7 sc. [18 sts]

Round 2: BLO 1 sc in each st. [18 sts]

Rounds 3–7: 1 sc in each st. [18 sts]

Round 8: 1 reverse sc in each st and do not fasten off. [18 sts]

Ch 50 to create the strap, and join with a sl st on the opposite side of the Bag.

Fasten off and weave in the yarn.

Place the Mushrooms in the Bag, and slip the Bag over her shoulder.

CHAPTER 5

Hazel the Forest Fairy

SKILL LEVEL: SPRINKLE

Hazel is the forest's tiny caretaker, known for her beanie hats and see-through brown wings that flutter like dragonflies. Her favorite thing to do is sit under a hollowed-out log and chat with her toad companions. She spends her days watching over every quiet corner of the forest and makes sure it flourishes with life throughout the seasons.

Finished Height:

- 9" (22.9cm)

Tools and Materials:

- US C/2 (2.75mm) and US 8/7/2 (1.5mm) crochet hooks
- Two 6mm safety eyes
- Basic Craft Supplies (page 12)
- Basic Crochet Tools (page 11)

Yarn:

- YarnArt Jeans (Weight: #2 Fine)
    - Color 73 (Peach)—1 ball
    - Color 03 (Polar White)—1 ball
    - Color 05 (Ecru)—1 ball
    - Color 07 (Tan)—1 ball
    - Color 82 (Olive Green)—1 ball
    - Color 70 (Cocoa)—1 ball
    - Color 84 (Mustard)—1 ball
    - Color 46 (Light Gray)—1 ball

Pattern Notes:

- Follow the master fairy doll pattern (page 15) first before continuing with this pattern, using the following colors:
    - Legs—light gray and peach
    - Arms/Head—peach
    - Hair Wig—tan
    - Body—polar white and light gray
- Rounds are joined and not crocheted in spirals. At the end of each round, join with a slip stitch in the first stitch of that round, then chain 1.
- Use a US C/2 (2.75mm) crochet hook unless otherwise stated.
- If instructed to cut a piece of yarn, use 36" (91.4cm) unless otherwise stated.

Fig. 1

Fig. 2

HAIR

Picking up from Round 19 of the Hair Wig, move on to Round 20. Round 20 will create Hazel's hairstyle. Continue with the same color (tan):

Round 20:

- **Part 1**—(1 sc, 1 picot) 5 times, 1 sc, 1 hdc, 1 dc.
- **Part 2**—Ch 20, start in the 2nd ch from the hook, 3 sc in each ch (*Fig. 1*). Sl st into the starting dc from Part 1, 1 dc into the next st from Part 1, ch 10, start in the 2nd ch from the hook, 3 sc in each ch, sl st into the dc st from Part 1.
- **Part 3**—(1 sc, 1 picot) 7 times, 2 hdc, 3 dc, 1 hdc, 1 sc, 1 sl st, 2 dc, 1 dc inc, 2 dc, 1 hdc, (1 sc, 1 picot) 12 times.

Fasten off and leave a long tail for sewing. Sew the Hair to the top of the Head (*Fig. 2*).

Fig. 3

Fig. 4

Fig. 5

DRESS

Starting with the color olive green:

Round 1: In the FLO of Round 8 of the Body, 1 sc in each st (*Fig. 3*). [24 sts]

Round 2: 1 sc inc in each st. [48 sts]

Round 3: (1 sc, 1 sc inc) 24 times. [72 sts]

Round 4: 1 sc in each st. [72 sts]

Round 5: (2 sc, 1 sc inc) 24 times. [96 sts]

Rounds 6–8: 1 sc in each st, changing the color to a mix between olive green and cocoa (split the yarn in half with two strands from each color and combine the two colors) at the end of Round 8 (*Fig. 4*). [96 sts]

Round 9: 1 sc in each st, changing the color to cocoa at the end of the round. [96 sts]

Rounds 10–11: 1 sc in each st, changing the color to a mix between cocoa and mustard at the end of Round 11. [96 sts]

Round 12: 1 sc in each st, changing the color to mustard at the end of the round. [96 sts]

Rounds 13–14: 1 sc in each st. [96 sts]

Round 15: (Ch 2, sl st into the next st) in each st. [96 sts]

Fasten off and weave in the yarn (*Fig. 5*).

HAT

Using the color light gray, first start with the ribbed edge of the hat.

Fig. 6

Fig. 7

Fig. 8

Fig. 9

Fig. 10

RIBBING

Row 1: Ch 5, starting in the 2nd ch from the hook, 4 sc, ch 1, turn. [4 sts]

Rows 2–46: BLO 1 sc in each st, ch 1, turn (*Fig. 6*). [4 sts]

Join Row 1 to Row 46 with a sl st through the BLO of Row 46 and the FLO of Row 1 (*Fig. 7*).

Continue to work in the round. Join with a sl st to the 1st st at the end of each round, then ch 1.

BEANIE

Round 1: 1 sc into the top of each row of the ribbed edge (*Fig. 8*). [46 sts]

Rounds 2–14: 1 sc in each st. [46 sts]

Round 15: (2 sc, 1 sc dec) 11 times, 2 sc. [35 sts]

Fasten off and leave a tail for sewing.

Turn the piece inside out. Using a wide running stitch, sew through the last round and pull tight to close the top of the Hat (*Figs. 9 and 10*).

Fasten off and weave in the yarn. Turn the piece right side out.

Make a small pom-pom and sew it at the top of the Hat. Make and sew on a Flower and Leaves (optional).

FLOWER (Make 3)

Fig. 11

Use a US 8/7/2 (1.5mm) crochet hook. Split the color mustard in half into two strands at roughly 24" (61cm) long.

Round 1: 5 sc in MR. [5 sts]

Round 2: (Ch 2, 2 dc, ch 2, sl st into the same st, sl st into the next st) 5 times (*Fig. 11*).

Fasten off and leave a tail for sewing. Embellish with a French knot in the middle of the Flower made with the color cocoa. Sew to the front of the Dress.

LEAF (Make 5)

Use a US 8/7/2 (1.5mm) crochet hook. Split the color olive green in half into two strands at roughly 24" (61cm) long.

Ch 5, sl st in the 2nd ch from the hook, 1 sc, 1 hdc, 1 dc, ch 2, continuing onto the other side of the chain, 1 dc, 1 hdc, 1 sc, 1 st.

Fasten off and leave a tail for sewing.

WINGS

Using the color cocoa:

BASE OF THE WINGS

Round 1: Ch 3, this will count as your 1st dc. [2 dc, ch 2, (3 dc, ch 2) 3 times] in the 1st chain, join to the top of the 1st ch-3 sp, ch 1, turn. [12 dc, 4 ch-2 sp]

Do not fasten off.

PRIMARY WING (MAKE 2)

Now working in rows, continue from the pattern of the Base:

Row 2: Working around both strands of wire, 49 sc, curve the wire, and sl st into the next ch-2 sp, ch 1, turn (*Figs. 12 and 13*).

Row 3: 1 sc in each st around the Wing, sl st into the ch-2 sp, ch 1, turn (*Figs. 14 and 15*). [50 sts]

Row 4: *3 sl st, ch 16, sl st into a st on the opposite side of the Wing*, repeat from * to * 3 more times, alternating back and forth and from side to side to create a unique crisscross design (*Figs. 16 and 17*).

Fasten off and weave in the yarn.

SECONDARY WING (MAKE 2)

Refer to the Secondary Wing pattern (page 22). Attach each Wing to the Base. Sew the Wings to the back of the Body.

Fig. 12

Fig. 13

Fig. 14

Fig. 15

Fig. 16

Fig. 17

CHAPTER 5

Toad Friends

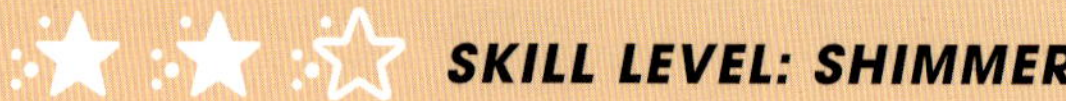

The woodland fairies share a special bond with their toad companions, who are more than just friends; they are trusted helpers. The toads handle earthy tasks like turning soil with their strong legs or carrying dewdrops to other plants in the forest. They croak cheerful tunes and nudge sleepy fairies with their wart-filled heads when they are needed. Loyal, clever, and somewhat clumsy, these toads bring joy wherever they go.

Finished Height:
- 4" (10.2cm)

Tools and Materials:
- US C/2 (2.75mm) crochet hook
- Two 9mm safety eyes
- Basic Craft Supplies (page 12)
- Basic Crochet Tools (page 11)

Yarn:
- YarnArt Jeans (Weight: #2 Fine)
  - Brown Toad:
    - Color 07 (Tan)—1 ball
    - Color 70 (Cocoa)—1 ball
    - Color 82 (Olive Green)—1 ball
    - Color 53 (Black)—1 ball
  - Green Toad:
    - Color 29 (Bright Green)—1 ball
    - Color 92 (Bayou)—1 ball
    - Color 70 (Cocoa)—1 ball
    - Color 53 (Black)—1 ball

Pattern Notes:
- Rounds are joined and not crocheted in spirals. At the end of each round, join with a slip stitch in the first stitch of that round, then chain 1.
- Yarn colors are given for the green toad, with the brown toad yarn shown in parentheses.
- If instructed to cut a piece of yarn, use 36" (91.4cm) unless otherwise stated.

Fig. 1

Fig. 2

HEAD

Starting with the color bright green (tan):

Round 1: Ch 7, 1 sc inc in the 2nd ch from the hook, 4 sc, 4 sc in the last ch, rotate the piece to work along the opposite side of the foundation ch, 4 sc, 1 sc inc (*Fig. 1*). [16 sts]

Round 2: 1 sc inc, 6 sc, 2 sc inc, 6 sc, 1 sc inc. [20 sts]

Round 3: 1 sc in each st. [20 sts]

Round 4: 1 sc, 1 sc inc, 7 sc, 1 sc inc, 1 sc, 1 sc inc, 7 sc, 1 sc inc. [24 sts]

Round 5: 1 sc in each st. [24 sts]

Round 6: 2 sc, 1 sc inc, 6 sc, 1 sc inc, 4 sc, 1 sc inc, 6 sc, 1 sc inc, 2 sc. [28 sts]

Rounds 7–8: 1 sc in each st. [28 sts]

Round 9: 2 sc dec, 6 sc, 4 sc dec, 6 sc, 2 sc dec. [20 sts]

Round 10: (2 sc, 1 sc dec) 5 times. [15 sts]

Round 11: (1 sc, 1 sc dec) 5 times. [10 sts]

Begin stuffing the head.

Round 12: (5 sc dec) 5 times. [5 sts]

Fasten off and weave in the yarn (*Fig. 2*).

Fig. 3

BODY

Starting with the color bright green (tan):

Round 1: 6 sc in MR. [6 sts]

Round 2: 1 sc inc in each st. [12 sts]

Round 3: (1 sc, 1 sc inc) 6 times. [18 sts]

Round 4: (2 sc, 1 sc inc) 6 times. [24 sts]

Round 5: (3 sc, 1 sc inc) 6 times. [30 sts]

Rounds 6–7: 1 sc in each st. [30 sts]

Round 8: (1 sc, 1 sc dec) 6 times. [24 sts]

Rounds 9–11: 1 sc in each st. [24 sts]

Round 12: (2 sc, 1 sc dec) 6 times. [18 sts]

Do not fasten off. Stuff the Body. Sew the Head to the Body, continuing to stuff as you go (*Fig. 3*).

EYE (Make 2)

FRONT OF THE EYE

Starting with the color bright green (tan):

Row 1: Ch 5, start in the 2nd ch from the hook, 1 sc in each st, ch 1, turn. [4 sts]

Row 2: 1 sc in each st, ch 1, turn. [4 sts]

Row 3: 2 sc dec. [2 sts]

Fasten off. Insert the safety eyes in the center of the front of the Eye.

Fig. 4

BACK OF THE EYE

Starting with the color bayou (cocoa):

Make the same as the Front of the Eye.

- Hold both Front and Back together, 9 sc around through both layers (*Fig. 4*), and stuff the eye lightly as you work.

FINISHING

Fig. 5

Sew the Eyes to the Head in Rounds 1–3 (*Fig. 5*).

Using the color bayou (cocoa), add warts to the toad's face around the Eyes using French knots.

Using the color black, embroider a smile below the Eyes.

ARM (Make 2)

Starting with the color bright green (tan):

Round 1: 6 sc in MR. [6 sts]

Round 2: (1 sc, 1 sc inc) 3 times. [9 sts]

Round 3: 1 sc, 1 sc dec, 3 sl st, 1 sc dec, 1 sc. [7 sts]

Fig. 6

Rounds 4–7: 1 sc in each st. [7 sts]

Do not stuff the Arms but fold them in half, and join the edges with 3 sc. Fasten off and leave a tail for sewing.

Sew the Arms to the Body at Round 11 of the Body, making sure the sl sts that shape the hand face forward (*Fig. 6*).

LEG (Make 2)

Fig. 7

Fig. 8

Starting with the color bright green (tan):

Round 1: 8 sc in MR. [8 sts]

Round 2: (1 sc, 1 sc inc) 4 times. [12 sts]

Round 3: 1 sc in each st. [12 sts]

Round 4: 2 sc, 1 sc dec, 4 sl st, 1 sc dec, 2 sc. [10 sts]

Round 5: 3 sc, 2 sc dec, 3 sc. [8 sts]

Stuff only the bottom of the Leg to create the feet.

Rounds 6–9: 1 sc in each st. [8 sts]

Fasten off and leave a tail for sewing. Fold the Leg in half. Using whipstitches, sew the top closed (*Fig. 7*).

Sew the Leg between Rounds 5–7 of the Body. Place a stitch in the center of the Leg next to the front of the Body to anchor it to the Body (*Fig. 8*).

VEST

Fig. 9

Starting with the color cocoa (olive green):

Row 1: Ch 20, starting in the 2nd ch from the hook, 19 sc, ch 1, turn. [19 sts]

Row 2: 1 sc, 1 sc inc, ch 3, skip 3 sts, 1 sc inc, 7 sc, 1 sc inc, ch 3, skip 3 sts, 1 sc inc, 1 sc, ch 1, turn. [23 sts]

Row 3: 3 hdc, 3 hdc along the ch-3 sp, 11 hdc, 3 hdc around the ch 3, 3 hdc, ch 1, turn. [23 sts]

Row 4: 1 hdc in each st (*Fig. 9*). [23 sts]

Fasten off and weave in the yarn. Place the Vest on the toad.

Chapter

6

Celestial Fairies and Their Firefly Friends

The celestial fairies are the quiet guardians of the night while the world sleeps. Phoebe keeps the moon shining and the tides moving while Stella fills the night sky with sparkling light. Together with their firefly friends, they watch over the night, keeping it full of magic and wonder and making sure all is calm and quiet.

CHAPTER 6

Stella the Star Fairy

SKILL LEVEL: SHIMMER

The Star Fairy can always be seen right when the sun sets for the day. As dusk settles, it is her duty to wake the stars one by one, coaxing them from their slumber with a gentle hum. When her work is done, the sky gleams with countless diamonds—and the world below dreams beneath her watchful, celestial care.

Finished Height:
- 9" (22.9cm)

Tools and Materials:
- US C/2 (2.75mm) and US 8/7/2 (1.5mm) crochet hooks
- Two 6mm safety eyes
- Basic Craft Supplies (page 12)
- Basic Crochet Tools (page 11)

Yarn:
- YarnArt Jeans (Weight: #2 Fine)
  - Color 73 (Peach)—1 ball
  - Color 03 (Polar White)—1 ball
  - Color 01 (White)—1 ball
  - Color 68 (Steel Blue)—1 ball
  - Color 54 (Flag Blue)—1 ball
  - Color 15 (Sky Blue)—1 ball
  - Color 55 (Capri)—1 ball
  - Color 28 (Dark Gray)—1 ball
  - Color 46 (Light Gray)—1 ball
  - Color 35 (Sunflower)—1 ball

Pattern Notes:
- Follow the master fairy doll pattern (page 15) first before continuing to this pattern, using the following colors:
  - Legs—flag blue and peach
  - Head/Arms—peach
  - Body—polar white and white
  - Hair Wig—dark gray
- Rounds are joined and not crocheted in spirals. At the end of each round, join with a slip stitch in the first stitch of that round, then chain 1.
- Use a US C/2 (2.75mm) crochet hook unless otherwise stated.
- If instructed to cut a piece of yarn, use 36" (91.4cm) unless otherwise stated.

SHOE FLAP

Fig. 1

Using the color steel blue, attach a sl st in the FLO of Round 9 of the Leg master pattern, at the back of the shoe, and continue as follows: 1 sc, 1 sl st, (1 hdc, 1 dc, 1 hdc) in the same st, 2 sl st, (1 hdc, 1 dc, 1 hdc) in the same st, 1 sl st, 3 sc.

Fasten off (*Fig. 1*).

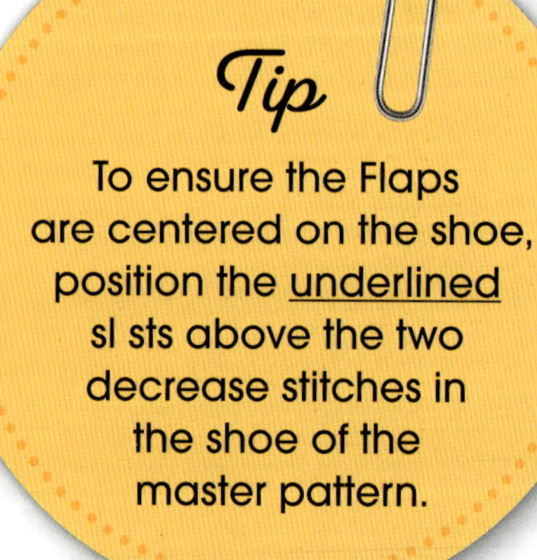

HAIR

Fig. 2

Fig. 3

Picking up from Round 19 of the Hair Wig, move on to Round 20. Round 20 will create Stella's hairstyle. Continue with the same color (dark gray):

Round 20:

- **Part 1**—Ch 1, skip 1st st, sl st in the next st, (ch 1, sl st) 17 times (*Fig. 2*).

- **Part 2**—Ch 5, starting in the 2nd ch from the hook, 4 sl st, sl st into the next st of Round 19, *ch 7, starting in the 2nd ch from the hook, 6 sl st, sl st in the next st of Round 19*, repeat from * to * 2 more times.
- **Part 3**—Sl st, ch 1, sl st in the next st.
- **Part 4**—Ch 5, starting in the 2nd ch from the hook, 4 sl st, sl st into the next st of Round 19*, repeat from * to * 1 more time.
- **Part 5**—(Ch 1, sl st) 18 times.

Fasten off and leave a tail for sewing. Sew the Wig to the Head, with the bangs in front, and sew them to the forehead, overlapping them as you stitch them down (*Fig. 3*).

HAIR BUN

Refer to Bramble the Autumn Fairy's pattern (page 32) for the Hair Bun. Sew it to the top of Stella's head, centered toward the back. Stuff the Bun lightly prior to sewing it onto the Head.

DRESS

Refer to Hazel the Forest Fairy's pattern (page 77) for the Dress. Use the following color sequence:

- **Rounds 1–3**. White.
- **Rounds 4–5**: Mix of white and capri (split the yarn in half with two strands from each color and combine the two colors).
- **Rounds 6–8**: Capri.
- **Round 9**: Mix of capri and sky blue.
- **Round 10**: Sky blue.
- **Round 11**: Mix of sky blue and steel blue.
- **Rounds 12–14**: Steel blue.
- **Round 15**: Mix steel blue and flag blue.

Change the color to flag blue only. Do not fasten off, but continue working the following rounds:

Rounds 16–18: 1 sc in each st. [96 sts]

Round 19: 1 hdc in ch st. [96 sts]

Round 20: Reverse sc st in each st. [96 sts]

Fasten off and weave in the yarn. Embellish the bottom of the Dress with two Stars, or more if you choose.

SHAWL

Using the color white, crochet in rows:

Row 1: Ch 35, starting in the 3rd ch from the hook, 33 hdc, ch 1, turn. [33 sts]

Row 2: BLO 33 sc in each st, ch 1, turn. [33 sts]

Row 3: 1 hdc in each st. [33 sts]

Fasten off and leave a tail for sewing.

Join the sides of the Shawl using a whipstitch. Place the Shawl over the doll's shoulders.

STAR (Make 5)

Fig. 4

Use a US 8/7/2 (1.5mm) crochet hook. Split the color sunflower in half into two strands.

Round 1: 5 sc in a MR. [5 sts]

Round 2: *Ch 3, 1 sl st in the 2nd ch from the hook, 1 sc, 1 sl st into the next st*, repeat from * to * 4 more times.

Fasten off and leave a tail for sewing (*Fig. 4*).

HAIR TIE

Using the color capri or sky blue, ch 30, attach a Star to the next ch, ch 5, attach another Star to the next ch, ch 75.

Fasten off. Make an overhand knot at each end. Wrap the Hair Tie around her Hair Bun, and tuck one end under the Bun.

NECKLACE

Use a US 8/7/2 (1.5mm) crochet hook. Split the color light gray in half. Ch 20, attach a Star to the next ch, and ch 20. Loop the Necklace around her neck and join to the 1st ch with a sl st and fasten off.

WINGS

BASE OF THE WINGS

Starting with the color white:

Round 1: 8 sc in MR. [8 sts]

Round 2: (1 sc, ch 2, 1 sc in next st) 4 times.

Fasten off.

LEFT PRIMARY WING

Fig. 5

Starting with the color sky blue:

Round 1: Ch 10, start in the 2nd ch from the hook, 1 sc inc, 7 sc, 3 sc in the last ch, rotate the piece to work along the opposite side of the foundation ch, 8 sc. [20 sts]

Round 2: 1 sc, 1 sc inc, 7 sc, 1 sc inc, 1 sc, 1 sc inc, 7 sc, 1 sc inc. [24 sts]

Round 3: 3 sc, 1 sc inc, 4 sc, 1 sc inc, 6 sc, 1 sc inc, 4 sc, 1 sc inc, 3 sc. [28 sts]

Round 4: 2 sc, 1 hdc, 1 hdc inc, 5 hdc, 1 dc, skip 2 sts, 8 dc in the next st, skip 2, 1 hdc inc, 12 hdc. [33 sts]

Insert the jewelry wire on this round:

Round 5: 3 sc, 1 sc inc, 8 sc, 4 hdc, (1 hdc, ch 1, 1 hdc) in the next st, 5 sc, ch 1, 12 sc. [36 sts]

Fasten off and leave a tail for sewing (*Fig. 5*).

RIGHT PRIMARY WING

Repeat Rounds 1–3 of the Left Primary Wing, and then continue as follows:

Round 4: 12 hdc, 1 hdc inc, skip 2 sts, 8 dc in the next st, skip 2 sts, 1 dc, 5 hdc, 1 hdc inc, 1 hdc, 2 sc. [33 sts]

Insert the jewelry wire on this round:

Round 5: 12 sc, ch 1, 5 sc, (1 hdc, ch 1, 1 hdc) in the next st, 4 hdc, 8 sc, 1 sc inc, 3 sc. [36 sts]

Fasten off and leave a tail for sewing.

SECONDARY WING (MAKE 2)

Refer to the Secondary Wing pattern (page 22) and use the color light gray.

Attach each Secondary Wing to the Base by aligning the 1st row of each Wing to the ch-2 sp of the Base. Sew the Wings to the back of the Body.

CHAPTER 6

Phoebe the Moon Fairy

SKILL LEVEL: SHIMMER

The Moon Fairy glides across the night sky, her soft silver wings catching the light as she carries a little lantern made from real moonlight. It's her job to keep the moon shining bright so travelers can find their way and the world doesn't become too dark. Each night, she makes sure the tides rise and fall just as they should, giving the ocean its gentle rhythm. Though small, she's steady and careful, taking great pride in her work.

Finished Height:
- 9" (22.9cm)

Tools and Materials:
- US C/2 (2.75mm) crochet hook
- Two 6mm safety eyes
- Basic Craft Supplies (page 12)
- Basic Crochet Tools (page 11)

Yarn:
- YarnArt Jeans (Weight: #2 Fine)
    - Color 73 (Peach)—1 ball
    - Color 03 (Polar White)—1 ball
    - Color 28 (Dark Gray)—1 ball
    - Color 46 (Light Gray)—1 ball
    - Color 49 (Pearl Gray)—1 ball

Pattern Notes:
- Follow the master fairy doll pattern (page 15) first before continuing to this pattern, using the following colors:
    - Arms/Head—peach
        - When working the Arm, follow the master pattern up to Round 12.
    - Legs—dark gray and peach
    - Body—polar white and light gray
        - When working the Body, follow the master pattern up to Round 13.
    - Hair Wig—polar white
- Rounds are joined and not crocheted in spirals. At the end of each round, join with a slip stitch in the first stitch of that round, then chain 1.
- If instructed to cut a piece of yarn, use 36" (91.4cm) unless otherwise stated.

ARM (Make 2)

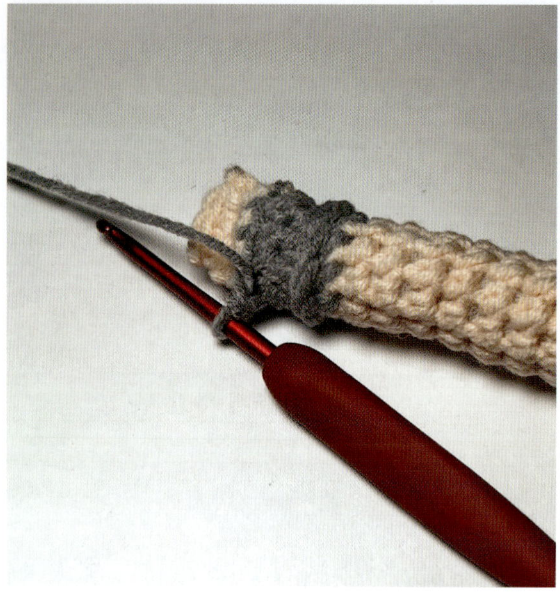

Fig. 1

Picking up from Round 12 of the Arm, move on to Round 13. Change to the color light gray at the end of Round 12.

Round 13: 1 sc in each st. [8 sts]

Round 14: BLO 1 sc in each st. [8 sts]

Round 15: 1 sc in each st, changing the color to peach at the end of the round. [8 sts]

Round 16: BLO 1 sc in each st. [8 sts]

Flatten the Arm and work 3 sc through both layers to close the Arm. Fasten off and weave in the yarn.

In the FLO of Rounds 14 and 16: 1 sl st in each st (*Fig. 1*).

BODY

Picking up from Round 13 of the Body, move on to Round 14. Change to the color peach at the end of Round 13.

Round 14: BLO 1 sc in each st. [16 sts]

Rounds 15–17: Follow the master pattern to finish the Body. Do not use BLO in Round 16.

HAIR

Fig. 2

Picking up from Round 19 of the Hair Wig, move on to Round 20. Round 20 will create Phoebe's hairstyle. Continue with the same color (polar white):

Round 20:

- **Part 1**—(Ch 1, sl st in the next st) 12 times.

- **Part 2**—*[Ch 8, 1 sl st into the 2nd ch from the hook, 1 sc inc, 1 sc, 1 sc inc, 2 sc, sl st in the next st, ch 1, sl st in the next st] 3 times.*
- **Part 3**—Sl st in the next st (1 hdc, ch 1) 6 times, 2 sl st, (1 hdc, ch 1) 4 times.
- **Part 4**—Repeat from * to *
- **Part 5**—(Ch 1, sl st in the next st) 9 times.

Fasten off and leave a long tail for sewing. Sew the Wig to the Head (*Fig. 2*).

PONYTAIL

Round 1: 8 sc in MR. [8 sts]

Round 2: 1 sc inc in BLO in each st. [16 sts]

Round 3: BLO 1 sc in each st, ch 1. [16 sts]

Moving up to the FLO of Round 3: *Ch 15, starting in the 2nd ch from the hook, (3 sc, in the next ch, 1 sc) 6 times, 1 sc, skip 1 FLO st, 1 sl st in the next FLO st of Round 3*. Repeat from * to * 7 more times, and then ch 1.

Moving up to the FLO of Round 2: Repeat from * to * 4 times.

Fasten off and leave a tail for sewing. Sew the Ponytail to the top of the Head toward the back.

DRESS

Refer to Hazel the Forest Fairy's pattern (page 77) for the Dress. Use the color light gray for all rounds. You do not need to blend any colors together. Do not fasten off, but continue working the following rounds:

Rounds 16–18: 1 sc in each st. [96 sts]

Round 19: 1 hdc in each st. [96 sts]

Round 20: Reverse sc st in each st. [96 sts]

Fasten off and weave in the yarn.

TOP OF THE DRESS

From Round 14 of the Body: FLO (sl st, ch 1) in each st.

Fasten off and weave in the yarn.

MOON CRATERS

Fig. 3

To create the look of moon craters on the Dress, create as many of the following pattern as desired (*Fig. 3*). Use the color light gray for all Craters.

Small Crater (Make 2): Ch 10 and sew onto the Dress in a circle in random places.

Medium Crater (Make 2): Ch 15 and sew onto the Dress in a circle in random places.

Large Crater (Make 3): Ch 20 and sew onto the Dress in a circle in random places.

CHOKER NECKLACE

Using the color dark gray: Ch 15, starting in the 2nd ch from the hook, 14 sc along the ch.

Fasten off. Wrap the Choker around the neck and sew the ends together.

WINGS

Refer to Stella the Star Fairy's pattern (page 96) for the Wings. Use the color pearl gray for all rounds.

Sew the Wings to the back of the Body.

MOON LANTERN

Starting with the color polar white:

Round 1: 6 sc in a MR. [6 sts]

Round 2: 1 sc inc in each st. [12 sts]

Round 3: (1 sc, 1 sc inc) 6 times. [18 sts]

Round 4: (2 sc, 1 sc inc) 6 times. [24 sts]

Rounds 5–7: 1 sc in each st. [24 sts]

Round 8: (2 sc, 1 sc dec) 6 times. [18 sts]

Round 9: (1 sc, 1 sc dec) 6 times. [12 sts]

Round 10: 6 sc dec. [6 sts]

Fasten off.

HANDLE

Using the color dark gray, ch 14.

Fasten off and leave a tail for sewing. Attach the ch to the top of the Moon Lantern by sewing each end to the sides, near the top. Place the Lantern over one of her hands.

CHAPTER 6

Firefly Friends

SKILL LEVEL: SHIMMER

When night falls, the firefly friends awaken like tiny lanterns flickering around in the night. They flutter up from the meadows to help the celestial fairies with their nightly work, carrying bits of starlight in their glowing bellies. They whisper secrets to the stars and chase each other through the clouds, leaving twinkling patterns in their wake. Together, they make the night sparkle—a perfect mix of fairy magic and firefly mischief.

Finished Height:
- 3" (7.6cm)

Tools and Materials:
- US C/2 (2.75mm) crochet hook
- Two 6mm safety eyes
- Basic Craft Supplies (page 12)
- Basic Crochet Tools (page 11)

Yarn:
- YarnArt Jeans (Weight: #2 Fine)
    - Color 01 (White)—1 ball
    - Color 68 (Steel Blue)—1 ball
    - Color 54 (Flag Blue)—1 ball
    - Color 15 (Sky Blue)—1 ball
    - Color 55 (Capri)—1 ball
    - Color 46 (Light Gray)—1 ball
    - Color 35 (Sunflower)—1 ball

Pattern Notes:
- Rounds are joined and not crocheted in spirals. At the end of each round, join with a slip stitch in the first stitch of that round, then chain 1.
- If instructed to cut a piece of yarn, use 36" (91.4cm) unless otherwise stated.

BODY

Starting with the color flag blue:

Round 1: 6 sc in a MR. [6 sts]

Round 2: 1 sc inc in each st. [12 sts]

Round 3: (1 sc, 1 sc inc) 6 times. [18 sts]

Round 4: 1 sc in each st. [18 sts]

Round 5: (2 sc, 1 sc inc) 6 times. [24 sts]

Round 6: 1 sc in each st, changing the color to a mix between flag blue and steel blue (split the yarn in half with two strands from each color and combine the two colors) at the end of the round. [24 sts]

Round 7: 1 sc in each st, changing the color to steel blue at the end of the round. [24 sts]

Round 8: 1 sc in each st, changing the color to a mix between steel blue and sky blue at the end of the round. [24 sts]

Round 9: 1 sc in each st, changing the color to sky blue at the end of the round. [24 sts]

Round 10: 1 sc in each st, changing the color to a mix between sky blue and capri at the end of the round. [24 sts]

Round 11: 1 sc in each st, changing the color to capri at the end of the round. [24 sts]

Round 12: 1 sc in each st, changing the color to a mix between capri and white at the end of the round. [24 sts]

Round 13: 1 sc in each st, changing the color to white at the end of the round. [24 sts]

Round 14: 1 sc in each st. [24 sts]

Round 15: (2 sc, 1 sc dec) 6 times. [18 sts]

Rounds 16–17: 1 sc in each st. [18 sts]

Round 18: (1 sc, 1 sc dec) 6 times. [12 sts]

Fasten off and leave the Body open to attach the Head.

Embroider the bottom of the Body with the color sunflower, using small stitches to resemble stars. Stuff the Body.

HEAD

Starting with the color white:

Round 1: 6 sc in a MR. [6 sts]

Round 2: 1 sc inc in each st. [12 sts]

Round 3: (1 sc, 1 sc inc) 6 times. [18 sts]

Round 4: (2 sc, 1 sc inc) 6 times. [24 sts]

Rounds 5–9: 1 sc in each st. [24 sts]

Place the eyes between Rounds 8 and 9 about 5 sts apart.

Round 10: (2 sc, 1 sc dec) 6 times. [18 sts]

Round 11: (1 sc, 1 sc dec) 6 times. [12 sts]

Fasten off and leave a long tail for sewing. Stuff the Head, then sew the Head to the Body, continuing to stuff as you sew.

ANTENNA (Make 2)

ANTENNA TOPPER

Starting with the color sky blue:

Round 1: 4 sc in a MR. [4 sts]

Round 2: (1 sc, 1 sc inc) 2 times.

Round 3: (1 sc, 1 sc dec) 2 times.

Fasten off and weave in the yarn.

ANTENNA BASE

Fold a short piece of jewelry wire (about 4" [10.2cm]) in half. Using the color flag blue, work 10 sc around the wire. Join with a sl st to the 1st sc to make a closed circle.

Bend the Base into an oval shape, sew the Topper to one end, and sew the whole piece to the top of the Head.

WINGS

BASE OF THE WINGS

Refer to Stella the Star Fairy's pattern (page 96) for the Base. Use the color sky blue for all rounds.

PRIMARY WING (MAKE 4)

You will use the following pattern for both the Primary and Secondary Wings of the firefly. Make 2 using the color sky blue and 2 using the color light gray:

Round 1: Ch 9, starting on the 2nd ch from the hook, 1 sc inc, 6 sc, 3 sc in the last ch, rotate the piece to continue along the opposite side of the foundation ch, 7 sc, ch 1. Do not join. [18 sts]

From here, you will work in rows. Turn your work. Sew the Wings to the back of the Body.

Row 2: 7 sc, 1 sc inc, 1 sc, 1 sc inc, 7 sc, ch 1, turn. [19 sts]

Row 3: 8 hdc, 3 hdc inc, 8 hdc, ch 1, turn. [22 sts]

Insert the wire on this row:

Row 4: 8 sc, 1 sc inc, 4 sc, 1 sc inc, 8 sc, do not turn. [24 sts]

Short Edge:

- Rotate the piece 90 degrees clockwise, 1 sc dec, 2 sc, 1 sc dec, ch 1, turn. [4 sts]
- 2 sc dec and fasten off. [2 sts]

Sew the Wings to the back of the Body.

Basic Crochet Stitches

No matter how experienced you are, having a quick reference for stitches and abbreviations is always useful. The following basic stitches and techniques are used in many amigurumi projects, and you will find all the basic stitches you need as you work through the patterns.

Crochet Abbreviations

ABBREVIATION	MEANING
BLO	back loop only
Bo	bobble
ch(s)	chain(s)
ch sp	chain space
cm	centimeter(s)
dc	double crochet
dec	decrease
FLO	front loop only
FP	front post stitches
FPsc	front post single crochet
hdc	half double crochet
inc	increase
m	meter(s)
mm	millimeter(s)
MR	magic ring
oz	ounce(s)
reverse sc	reverse single crochet
sc	single crochet
sl st	slip stitch
sp(s)	space(s)
st(s)	stitch(es)
tr	treble
yd(s)	yard(s)
"	inch(es)
*****	repeat as directed
[] or ()	repeat as directed

Stitch Glossary

SLIP KNOT

1

Pick up the yarn and wrap it once around two fingers, making sure it crosses over to form an X. Use your thumb to hold the yarn end.

2

With the hook, go under the first strand and over the second. Pull a loop. The yarn will twist and create a loose loop on the hook.

3

Slide your fingers out of the ring while keeping the loop on the hook.

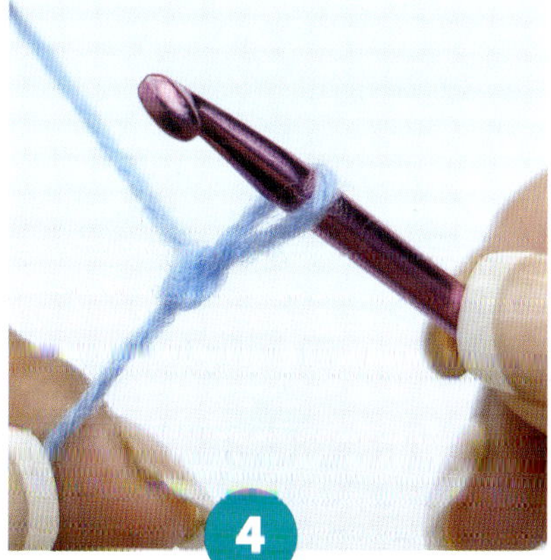

4

Grab the yarn end between your thumb and middle finger while holding the other side of the yarn over your forefinger. Tighten the loop around the hook.

5

The slip knot is now complete. You can adjust how tight the loop sits around the hook by pulling the tail.

MAGIC RING (MR)

The magic ring is often used to start an amigurumi project or a crochet project that is being crocheted in the round, such as granny squares or doilies.

Follow steps 1 and 2 of Slip Knot.

1

2

Go over the first loop and under the second one. Pull a loop through the loop on the hook.

3

Slide your fingers out of the ring while keeping the loop on the hook.

YARN OVER & YARN UNDER

Yarn over and yarn under are ways to pick up the yarn with your hook to pull it through the loops on your hook. Depending on the result you want to achieve, you might want to use one of these two techniques.

The yarn under method is not used often, mostly to crochet the amigurumi single crochet stitches, while the yarn over method is used widely to create the basic stitches.

YARN OVER

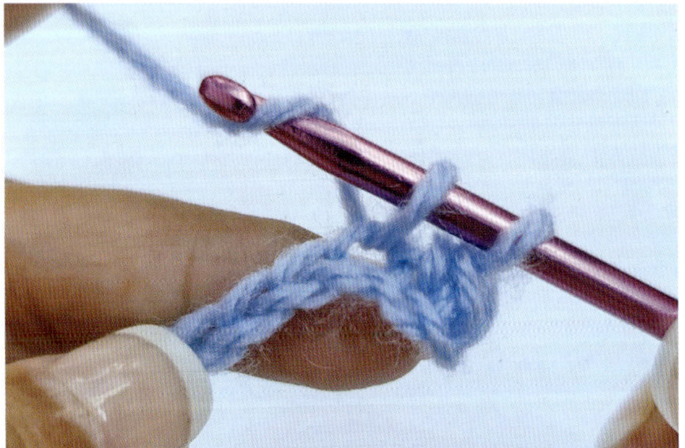

Bring the hook in front of the yarn. Wrap the yarn over the hook from back to front (in between the loops on the hook and the throat of the hook).

YARN UNDER

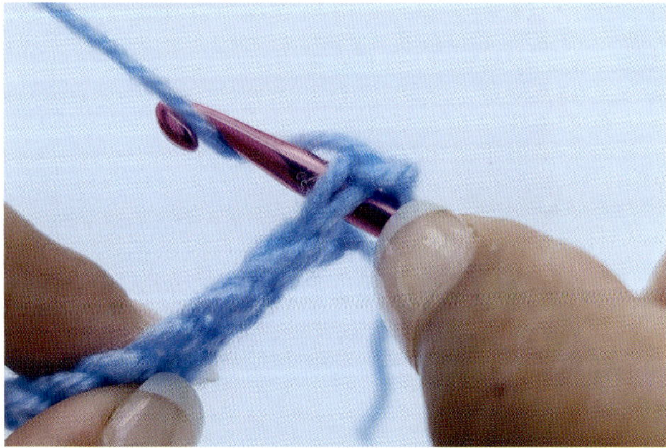

Bring the hook over the yarn so that the yarn just catches on the hook.

CHAIN (CH)

The chain has multiple uses:

- To create the first row of a crochet project, called the foundation chain.
- To replace some of the basic stitches, mostly at the beginning of the rows (ch 2 for a half double crochet, ch 3 for a double crochet, ch 4 for a treble).
- To make a basic stitch in the construction of a crochet pattern. For example, in patterns that use picot stitches or in patterns that skip stitches.

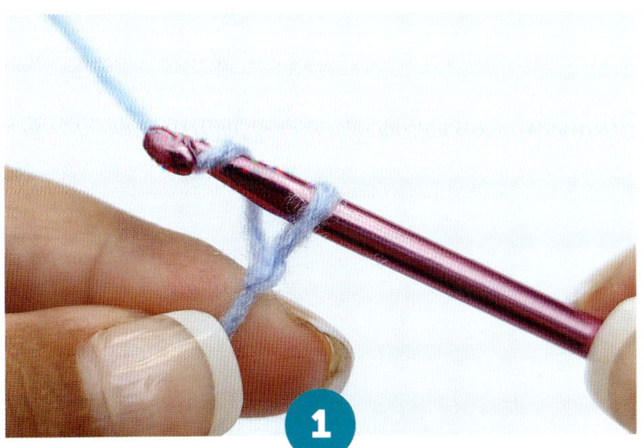

Start with a slip knot. Yarn over and pull the loop through the loop on the hook.

2 The chain is complete. Repeat as many times as instructed.

FOUNDATION CHAIN

This refers to a sequence of chain stitches beginning with a slip knot into which you work the first row of stitches.

CHAIN SPACE (CH SP)

Whenever you are making chains in a crochet pattern (except the foundation chains), you will create a space between rows. This is called a chain space.

When instructed to crochet stitches in the chain space (often the number of chains are mentioned; for example, chain two space = ch-2 sp), you need to insert the hook into that space and crochet your stitches around the chains. Don't insert the hook into the actual chain.

SKIP

In crochet, you will work your stitch in the next available stitch below. When the pattern tells you to skip, you will pass the number of stitches as instructed and work your stitches from that point onward.

SINGLE CROCHET (SC)

The single crochet stitch is one of the most versatile basic stitches, commonly used for creating a tight and dense fabric.

Insert the hook into the next available chain or stitch (as directed in the pattern).

Yarn over and pull up a loop. You will have two loops on the hook.

Yarn over again and pull up a loop through both loops on the hook.

AMIGURUMI SINGLE CROCHET

The amigurumi single crochet is also known as the X-stitch single crochet because of its X-shaped stitches. It is widely used in amigurumi because of the tight fabric it creates. This allows crocheted pieces to be firmly stuffed with polyester fiber filling without stretching the stitches.

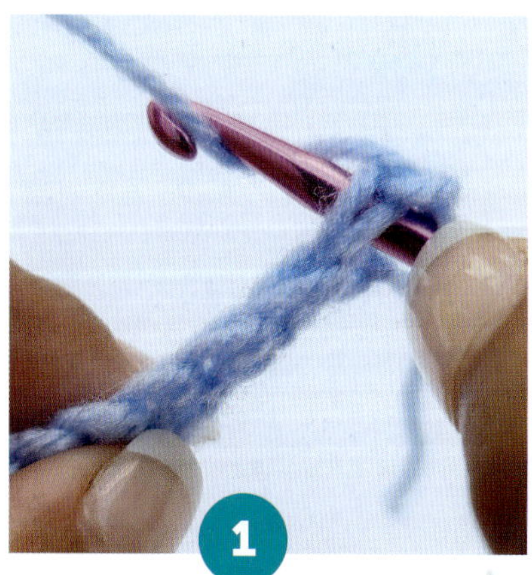

Insert the hook into the next available chain or stitch (as directed in the pattern).

Yarn under and pull up a loop. You will have two loops on the hook.

Yarn over again and pull up a loop through both loops on the hook.

REVERSE SINGLE CROCHET (REVERSE SC)

With a reverse single crochet, you are crocheting in the opposite direction from how you started your work. If your work was crocheted to the left, a reverse single crochet will be crocheted to the right.

The following instructions demonstrate if you started your crochet working from the right to the left:

Chain one. Insert the hook from the front to the back in the next stitch to the right.

Yarn over and pull up a loop. Yarn over again and pull it through both loops on the hook.

Continue, moving to the next stitch to the right.

HALF DOUBLE CROCHET (HDC)

A half double crochet is a basic crochet stitch that falls between a single crochet and a double crochet in terms of height and length. It creates a slightly taller stitch than a single crochet but shorter than a double crochet.

Yarn over and insert the hook into the next available chain or stitch (as directed in the pattern).

Yarn over again and pull through a loop. You will have three loops on the hook.

Yarn over and pull through all three loops on the hook.

DOUBLE CROCHET (DC)

A double crochet stitch is slightly taller than a half double crochet and shorter than a treble. It creates a fabric with more openness and height compared to single and half double crochet stitches. They allow you to work up projects more quickly due to their height.

Yarn over and insert the hook into the next available chain or stitch (as directed in the pattern).

Yarn over and pull through a loop. You will have three loops on the hook.

Yarn over and pull through the first two loops on the hook. You will have two loops left on the hook.

Yarn over and pull through both loops on the hook.

TREBLE (TR)

A treble is a taller and longer crochet stitch than both the double crochet and the half double crochet. It creates a more open and airy fabric, making it ideal for projects where a lacy or lightweight texture is desired.

1 Yarn over twice and insert the hook into the next available chain or stitch (as directed in the pattern).

2 Yarn over and pull up a loop. You will have four loops on the hook.

3 Yarn over and pull through the first two loops on the hook. You will have three loops on the hook.

4 Yarn over and pull through the first two loops on the hook. You will have two loops left on the hook.

5 Yarn over and pull through the first two loops on the hook.

INCREASE (INC)

Increasing in amigurumi simply means crocheting two single crochet stitches in the same stitch. This increases the stitch count of the round by one.

Note: Instead of a sc, use a hdc or dc when the instructions indicate hdc inc or dc inc.

DECREASE (DEC)

Decreasing in amigurumi means you are turning two stitches into one. This decreases the stitch count of the round by one.

Note: Instead of a sc, use a hdc when the instructions indicate hdc dec.

Insert the hook in the next available stitch, yarn over, and pull up a loop. You will have two loops on the hook.

Insert the hook into the next available stitch and pull up another loop. You will have three loops on the hook.

Yarn over and pull through all three loops on the hook.

SLIP STITCH (SL ST)

The slip stitch is the shortest of all basic stitches, and it's mainly used to close rounds in amigurumi or when crocheting motifs.

Insert the hook into the next available stitch and yarn over.

Pull up a loop through the stitch and through the loop on the hook.

BACK LOOP ONLY (BLO)

A stitch has a front and back loop that meet at one end to look like a horizontal V. To crochet a stitch in the back loop only means you insert the hook under the stitch loop that is farther away from you and crochet your stitch as usual.

This leaves the front loops to be exposed, creating a ridge at the front of your work where you can crochet another row of stitches.

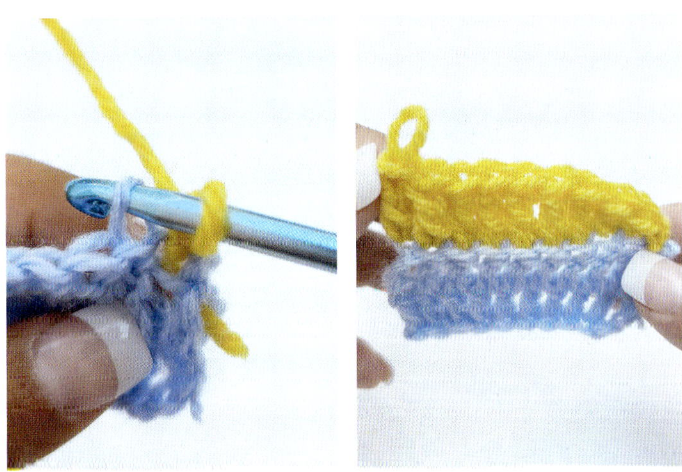

SINGLE CROCHET IN THE BACK LOOP ONLY (BLO SC)

Insert the hook through the back loop only of the next available stitch, yarn over, and pull up a loop. You will have two loops on the hook.

Yarn over and pull through both loops on the hook.

HALF DOUBLE CROCHET IN THE BACK LOOP ONLY (BLO HDC)

Yarn over, insert the hook through the back loop only of the next available stitch, yarn over, and pull up a loop. You will have three loops on the hook.

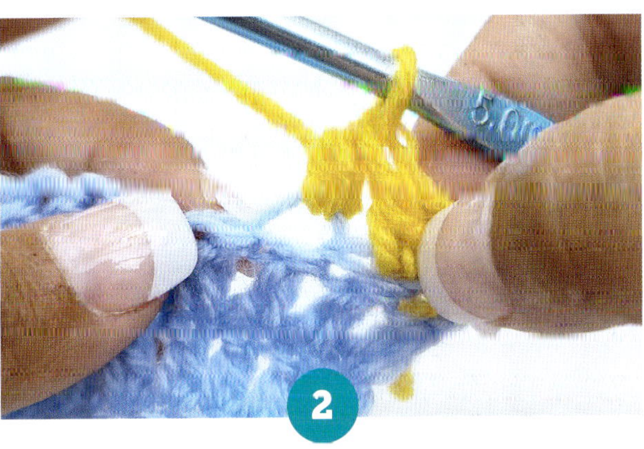

Yarn over and pull through all loops on the hook.

DOUBLE CROCHET IN THE BACK LOOP ONLY (BLO DC)

Yarn over, insert the hook through the back loop only of the next available stitch, yarn over, and pull up a loop. You will have three loops on the hook.

Yarn over and pull through the first two loops on the hook. You will have two loops left on the hook.

Yarn over and pull through the two remaining loops on the hook.

FRONT LOOP ONLY (FLO)

A stitch has a front and back loop that meet at one end to look like a horizontal V. To crochet a stitch in the front loop only means you insert the hook under the stitch loop that is closer to you and crochet your stitch as usual.

This will result in the back loops being left exposed, creating a ridge at the front of your work where you can crochet another row of stitches.

SINGLE CROCHET IN THE FRONT LOOP ONLY (FLO SC)

Insert the hook through the front loop only of the next available stitch, yarn over, and pull up a loop. You will have two loops on the hook.

Yarn over and pull through both loops on the hook.

HALF DOUBLE CROCHET IN THE FRONT LOOP ONLY (FLO HDC)

Yarn over, insert the hook through the front loop only of the next available stitch, yarn over, and pull up a loop. You will have three loops on the hook.

Yarn over and pull through all loops on the hook.

DOUBLE CROCHET IN THE FRONT LOOP ONLY (FLO DC)

Yarn over, insert the hook through the front loop only of the next available stitch, yarn over, and pull up a loop. You will have three loops on the hook.

Yarn over and pull through the first two loops on the hook. You will have two loops left on the hook.

Yarn over and pull through the two remaining loops on the hook.

FRONT POST STITCHES (FP)

This stitch is made up of two parts: the top part, called the loop (looks like a horizontal V), and the bottom part, called the stitch post (looks like a pillar and creates the actual body of the fabric). Front post stitches are stitches that are worked, from the front, around the stitch posts below instead of through the top loops of the stitches.

These stitches are usually used in crochet patterns to create raised textures, cables, or ribbing effects.

FRONT POST SINGLE CROCHET (FPSC)

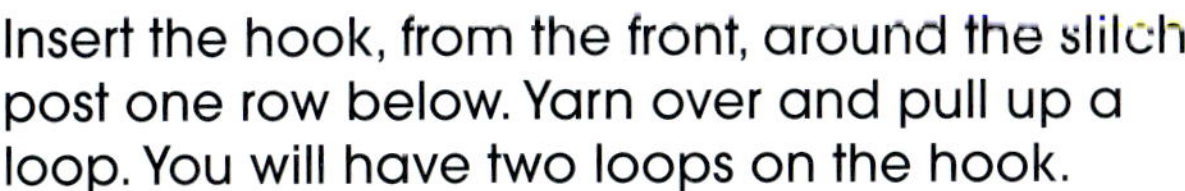
Insert the hook, from the front, around the stitch post one row below. Yarn over and pull up a loop. You will have two loops on the hook.

Yarn over and pull through both loops on the hook.

PICOT

The picot stitch is a decorative crochet technique used to create small loops or points along the edge of a crochet project. There are many variations of this stitch, but the most common one is crocheted with a chain of three.

Chain three. Insert the hook, from the top, through the middle of the base stitch (the stitch from where you made the ch 3). Pick up the front loop and the loop next to it. You will have three loops on the hook.

Yarn over and pull a loop through all three loops on the hook.

BOBBLE (BO)

Bobbles are groups of incomplete double crochet stitches that are made into the same stitch or chain space and are joined at the top. The more incomplete double crochets you make, the more your bobble will pop up. The five double crochet bobble is the most common way of creating a bobble stitch.

To make an incomplete double crochet stitch: yarn over, insert your hook into the next available stitch, yarn over, and pull up a loop (three loops on your hook).

Yarn over and pull through two loops on your hook (two loops on your hook). Leave the incomplete double crochet stitch on your hook.

Repeat steps 1 and 2, creating four more incomplete double crochet stitches into the same stitch. You will have six loops on the hook.

Yarn over and pull through all the loops on the hook.

CHANGING COLORS

There are several ways of changing colors, and they each have their purpose. Here are three different ways to change colors depending on where the color change happens and if you are crocheting back and forth or in the round.

JOINING A NEW YARN COLOR

This technique is usually used when you have a completed piece of crochet on which you want to continue with a new color (e.g., when starting a border on a blanket).

Make a slip knot and take it off the hook. Insert the hook through the top stitch of your piece and then back into the slip knot.

Pull the slip knot through the stitch and chain one.

AT THE END OF THE ROW

This technique is used when crocheting patterns with different color rows, and you don't want to cut the yarn. Instead, you leave the old color yarn on the side and pick it up when you return (or when you carry the yarn along). It can also be used if you are joining a new yarn color and your piece is not fastened off (meaning you still have the loop on the hook).

Finish the row as usual by completing the last stitch. Pick up the new color yarn and pull a loop through the loop on the hook.

Pull the old color yarn to tighten the loop. Continue with the new color as directed.

IN AMIGURUMI PROJECTS

Because amigurumi pieces are crocheted in a spiral manner, colored stripes won't have a smooth transition. Here is a technique for changing colors that will give a smoother transition between colors. It is not perfect, but it's less visible than just changing colors midway through finishing a stitch.

1

Complete the last stitch in the old color. Take the loop off the hook. Insert the hook, from the back, through the next stitch. Pick up the loop, pulling it through.

2

Release the old color yarn. Pick up the new color and pull a loop through the loop on the hook. Pull the old color yarn to tighten the loop, then secure the new color yarn by chaining one.

3

Continue to make the stitches as directed.

Index

Meet the Author

As a senior learning experience designer, Amber Beaulieu has developed and delivered impactful training programs that enhance employee productivity and elevate the customer experience, contributing to a more engaged and high-performing workforce.

With a master's in adult education, focusing on instructional design, Amber's passion has always been using her creativity in everything she does. When she's not crafting immersive learning experience in the corporate world, she channels that same creative spark into crocheting adorable, whimsical characters that are loved by both kids and adults.

Her work has earned first place at the local Hebron Harvest Fair, and she regularly showcases her creations at artisan festivals throughout New England.

A Note from the Author

My journey into the world of crocheting started at a very young age when my grandmother would crochet blanket after blanket and give them to me, my parents, and friends. At that time, I did not focus on learning how to crochet, nor did I have much of an interest in it. Instead, I dabbled in all types of crafts and hobbies growing up. It was not until my later years that I decided to give crochet a try, and after completing my first blanket, I could not stop. My simple blankets turned into complex mandala-design blankets then into amigurumi, which is now an obsessive passion.

My amigurumi creatures started taking over every surface of my home, which led me to start selling them at local artisan shows. After experiencing the rewarding feeling of seeing people, especially children, light up when they connected with my work, I knew I was *hooked* for life, no pun intended.

This book is a true expression of my love for this art. I truly hope you have as much fun making these beautiful dolls as I have.

ACKNOWLEDGMENTS

Thank you to my husband and my family for standing beside me through this entire project. Your support, patience, and love made this book possible, and every pattern in these pages carries a bit of the warmth you bring into my life. I'm endlessly grateful for all of you.

Thank you for showing up to my shows, for cheering me on from behind tables stacked with yarn creatures, and for celebrating every new idea right along with me. Your encouragement has made room for my creativity to grow, even on the busiest or most uncertain days. This fairy world came to life because you believed in me, and I couldn't have made it without your steady support.